SELF-CONFIDENCE FOR BEGINNERS

Ultimate Guide to Increase Self-Discipline, Build Self-Confidence, Develop High Self-Esteem, and Realize Your Value

Elizabeth Wright

© Copyright 2020 by Elizabeth Wright. All right reserved.

The work contained herein has been produced with the intent to provide relevant knowledge and information on the topic on the topic described in the title for entertainment purposes only. While the author has gone to every extent to furnish up to date and true information, no claims can be made as to its accuracy or validity as the author has made no claims to be an expert on this topic. Notwithstanding, the reader is asked to do their own research and consult any subject matter experts they deem necessary to ensure the quality and accuracy of the material presented herein.

This statement is legally binding as deemed by the Committee of Publishers Association and the American Bar Association for the territory of the United States. Other jurisdictions may apply their own legal statutes. Any reproduction, transmission or copying of this material contained in this work without the express written consent of the copyright holder shall be deemed as a copyright violation as per the current legislation in force on the date of publishing and subsequent time thereafter. All additional works derived from this material may be claimed by the holder of this copyright.

The data, depictions, events, descriptions and all other information forthwith are considered to be true, fair and accurate unless the work is expressly described as a work of fiction. Regardless of the nature of this work, the Publisher is exempt from any responsibility of actions taken by the reader in conjunction with this work. The Publisher acknowledges that the reader acts of their own accord and releases the author and Publisher of any responsibility for the observance of tips, advice, counsel, strategies and techniques that may be offered in this volume.

TABLE OF CONTENTS

Introduction 1
Chapter 1 *Drop Your Old Mindset - What Self-Confidence Truly Means* 3
Chapter 2 *Moving Out Of Your Comfort Zone* 13
Chapter 3 *Dealing With Nervous Anxiety* 23
Chapter 4 *Stomping Out Your Inner Critic* 33
Chapter 5 *Building A Tougher Character* 43
Chapter 6 *It's Okay To Look After Yourself* 53
Conclusion 63
Description 64

INTRODUCTION

Congratulations on purchasing *Self-Confidence for Beginners,* and thank you for doing so.

Walk into any bookstore, and you'll find plenty of books of self-confidence. Browse online, and you'll find thousands of websites talking about self-confidence as they encourage us to be a more confident version of ourselves. You'll find audiobooks, ebooks, podcasts, YouTube videos, and more, all talking about the same subject. The art of self-confidence is talked about everywhere in our society.

Confidence seekers are everywhere. They may not openly talk about it, but most people you pass on the street or even people you know directly could be secretly searching for the key to becoming a more confident person. If you want the very best out of life in every single area of your life, then confidence is the only way to achieve that outcome. When you're confident, you like yourself more. People like you a lot more too. They respect you. They listen to what you have to say. Right now, you're either insecure, or you're confident. There is no in-between, and if you're reading this book, you're probably the first option. But that is okay because confidence is something that can always be fixed. Through this book, you are going to learn to become the confident person that you want to be.

Does being confident mean you're going to be perfect? Or that you're never going to make mistakes ever again. Not at all. You are always going to make mistakes at some point, because like everyone else, that is what we do as humans. We make mistakes. If mistakes didn't exist, how would we ever learn from them? Through this book, you are going to learn the core principles of becoming a more confident person. To attract anything you want in life, you need confidence. You could be the most good looking, talented person in the world, but if you don't have confidence on your side, nobody is going to notice. Why? Because you'll subconsciously always be trying to hide. To fade into the background and stay out of the spotlight.

Confidence can never come from external factors. It has to come from within. Confidence is such a vital aspect of living a successful, happier, and more fulfilled life because, without confidence, you can be sure that the dominant thoughts and emotions you will have are going to be *negative*. It might not be happening 24/7, but every now and then, you're going to feel unhappy, miserable, depressed, and frustrated with yourself and your life in general. If you're always carrying these negative thoughts and emotions with you, it's going to be very difficult for you to accomplish any goal in life. Let's do something to fix that right now.

There are plenty of books on this subject on the market; thanks again for choosing this one! Every effort was made to ensure it is full of as much useful information as possible; please enjoy!

CHAPTER 1
Drop Your Old Mindset - What Self-Confidence Truly Means

Why do we care so much about confidence? Why do we associate this trait with success? Of course, we all want to be successful, and therefore, we believe we need to be more confident to land that job, get that raise, build the business of our dreams, network like a pro, and so on. You might even be wondering if successful people become more confident, or whether confidence is something they gain along the way with every victory and years of experience.

Here's another intriguing question to ponder: *Can confidence be manipulated?* Is it possible to make someone feel more confident at the moment? Can we fake it until we make it? Yes, we can because luckily for us, confidence is a skill that we can build. It is a quality that we can cultivate through deliberate action and changes to your mindset. We're capable of incredible change when we put our minds to it. The person you are today is not the same person you were yesterday, a week ago or a month ago. The version of you today is not going to be the same version of you in the future. That's because you are changed and shaped by the experiences you go through. Change is an inevitable part of life, but the way you change is entirely up to you. You can choose to change for the better, to learn from your experiences, and to use them to improve. Or you can choose to let those experiences hold you back and affect your confidence.

What Is Confidence?

Each one of us has thoughts and feelings. These thoughts and feelings come and go as we go about our day. Confidence is a magnifier of your thoughts. Some people trust their thoughts and use them to their advantage. For example, some people believe they would be brilliant as an entrepreneur, so they do something about it, and they go after that dream of theirs. That's an example of what confidence can do.

Confidence is what separates those who are living happy and fulfilled lives from the ones who feel like their life is going nowhere. If you think about it, a lot of superior achievements throughout history were not solely based on brainpower or incredible talent alone. It was the strange buoyancy of the soul that surged these successful individuals forward. It was *confidence* that had an important role to play, yet it also happens to be a trait that is easily overlooked. This incredible life-changing skill is not something you're going to learn about in your high school textbooks. That would explain why so many people struggle to grasp an understanding of what this concept truly entails. Confidence isn't an innate part of a lot of people. Some people are born with a natural inclination for it, while other people have to work for it.

When you have the courage to accept and embrace your imperfections, that is how you know you're confident and comfortable in your own skin. When you realize that nothing is ever going to be perfect and all you can do is try your best, that's the moment you reach the confidence levels you need to chase after your dreams. Confidence begins with the ability to forgive yourself for the mistakes you make along the way to greatness instead of doing what so many people tend to do. Beat themselves up repeatedly over the mistakes they have made in the past. It is impossible to love yourself or even begin to feel remotely confident when there is an inner voice inside your head that keeps harping on the negative. If the negative things about yourself are the only thing you can focus on, you have very little hope of ever building up any kind of self-confidence.

Why We Lack the Self-Confidence We Need

It goes back thousands of years. Given the life people in the early civilizations lived back then, opportunities were few and far between. So very different from the world that we are living in today. Most of the people would never go beyond their current station or even leave the town they were born in. It became a survival mechanism to keep their heads down and work as a way to avoid the pain of disappointment by expecting and hoping that there was more to life than this. Despite how far we have come, we still carry a little bit of that legacy from the past. We're afraid of disappointment. We don't want to risk being hurt, and that makes hope feel dangerous.

In the world we live in today, we're subtly surrounded by subconscious messages that imply we shouldn't get our hopes too high. It could be in the form of parents or family members, perhaps even friends, colleagues, and other people we may know, who questioned the ideas we talked about. Statements like *"Are you sure you want to do that? That sounds difficult, you might fail if you try"* are examples of the kind of statements that, if exposed to for too long, can slowly chip away at our confidence. Still, we can't blame them entirely. They were merely voicing their concerns, and they did it with good intentions. Even more so when family and close friends are concerned. They say things like that because they don't want to see us fail. They want to protect us from getting hurt. We would probably try and do the same for our loved ones too.

Schools were not the most confidence-inducing experience. Schools rarely encourage you to think outside the box. They want you to be well-behaved, follow the rules, do your homework, study, and get the grades you need to get you into university. The peers we had in school may or may not have helped to either bolster your confidence or bring it crashing down. When you lack confidence, that is when fear becomes bigger than anything else, and it becomes the only thing that matters. It cripples you, paralyzes you because your fear has become so strong it gets to a point where it consumes you, and you become so afraid that you eventually become incapable of doing or reacting to anything.

What We Lack Will Be Our Downfall

Oh yes, a lack of confidence is sure to be your downfall. It invokes nothing but feelings of negativity within you, and it becomes impossible to feel happy or look at the brighter side of life when all you can focus on is how unhappy you feel. When you lack confidence, it becomes easier to see the worst qualities than it is to see the good things you can do. In some extreme cases, poor self-esteem can even lead to feelings of depression and anxiety.

Confidence is something that can be fixed, but first, you need to identify the signs that you might not be as confident as you would like (if you don't already know it):

- **You're Not Assertive Enough** - Struggling to voice your needs is a sign that you lack confidence. You're hesitant about speaking up because you don't want to appear too demanding. You feel awkward about asking for a well-deserved promotion or talking about how you need to feel more supported in your relationship with your significant other. Even though you have every right to voice your concerns and needs, you still hold back because, well, you're not confident enough. Despite knowing that speaking your mind is going to be in your best interest, you're still reluctant to do it. The problem with this approach is that you end up neglecting yourself, and that is never good since it leads to eventual resentment and frustration at the world and yourself. You are the only one who can look after your needs. If you don't do something about it, no one else will. If you don't learn to be confident, you're always going to end up prioritizing someone else's needs above your own. Assertiveness goes hand-in-hand with confidence because it reminds you that you are worthy and deserving. Your needs *matter* just as much as everyone else's.

- **You're Always Explaining Yourself** - Even when you don't need to, you have this need to explain yourself. Sometimes in a long and lengthy way. You always seem to explain your choices, justifying and apologizing if you feel like you might be letting someone down. This makes you an *Explainer*. An *Explainer* is someone who is always waiting for permission and seeking approval from others over the personal choices they want to make. *You don't have to do this;* you know that you don't. But you can't help yourself because, well, you're not confident enough to stand by your choices without feeling guilty. Maybe those explanations are an honest attempt on your part to try and connect to the other person, but it is still an indication that you lack confidence. The intense desire to be liked and approved of by others is the reason you feel the need to explain yourself. This makes you a *People Pleaser,* and if you don't build the confidence you need, you're always going to be bothered by what someone else thinks about you.

- **You Make Excuses When You Make Mistakes** - Do you catch yourself making excuses immediately after you've messed up? Did you make excuses when something didn't go your way? Confident people do not give excuses for their mistakes. For example, if you were sitting at the table having lunch with a friend and you accidentally bump your water glass, causing the water to spill all over the table, you would immediately say, *"I'm so sorry, I'm so tired today I'm not concentrating properly,"* or *"Sorry about that! The glass was too close to my elbow."* Confident people do not try to explain their mistakes because they know that *everyone* makes mistakes. It happens, and there's nothing wrong with that. You're only human, and you don't need to make excuses whenever you mess up by accident. A confident person would say, *"Sorry about that guys! I'll clean that up,"* and move on. That's confidence.

- **When You're Alone, You Pretend to Be Busy On Your Phone** - You're not busy, but you try to make it look like you are so you don't have to feel awkward about the fact that you're on your own. Do you tend to do this a lot? Especially at social events and when you're out in public by yourself. Sitting alone can feel awkward, but confident people don't mind because they don't worry about what other people think about them. So they're sitting alone, that's okay. Maybe they don't know everyone at the social event, that's okay too. They're perfectly comfortable enjoying their own company or striking up a conversation with someone new. That is what confidence can do for you.

- **Compliments Make You Uncomfortable** - How do you respond when someone offers you a compliment? Do you reply by saying thank you? Or make excuses again like *"No, not really, I'm not that good at it."* When someone offers you a compliment without you having to fish for it, most of the time they mean it. Unless they are trying to butter you up and make you feel good so you will be more inclined to say yes. But most of the time, compliments are sincere, and they are meant to make you feel good about yourself. When someone offers you a nice compliment, and you push back against that by making excuses or downplaying the compliment, that is a clear sign that you lack confidence. Compliments are a struggle for you; even a simple thank you seems difficult.

Is It the Same as Self-Esteem? Not Really

Confidence is often confused with self-esteem. The latter focuses on how much you *like yourself,* the way you feel about yourself, and whether you're happy with the current version of yourself. Confidence, on the other hand, is about how *self-assured* you are. Confidence and self-esteem are *not* the same things. You could be highly confident or doubtful in both a good or a bad assessment of yourself. Confidence and self-esteem may not be similar, but there is one thing they share in common. They are both counter-productive traits that will lead to inaction because you simply feel too awkward, shy, reluctant, and worse, you don't believe that you can achieve success. Therefore, you will let a lot of opportunities slip through your fingers, some opportunities which could have changed your life in a tremendous way because you didn't have enough courage to grab onto them and hold on tight with both hands. Without confidence or self-esteem, you never know what you could be missing out on, whether it is a potential chance to network for the betterment of your career, forge new friendships and even build important connections.

If you think you're afraid to fail, think about this: *A lack of confidence and self-esteem is going to lead to the one thing that you should be afraid of. Never attempting to go after what you want. That is what you should be afraid of.* Imagine if some of the people who have left legacies that last a lifetime was too afraid to try. What if Thomas Edison had been afraid to keep going because he failed a thousand times at making the lightbulb. We would have been forced to live in darkness for a longer period. Imagine if the Wright Brothers were afraid to build their first airplane because they were afraid they might fail and come crashing down. We might never have had the chance to travel the world in the plane if no one else besides the Wright Brothers thought about this idea. Many of the inventions and modern-day conveniences we enjoy today would not exist if their creators were afraid to go for what they wanted. The possibility of failure is always going to be there. But having the courage and confidence to go ahead and do it anyway despite the possibility of failure, that is the quality that makes self-confidence so remarkably life-changing.

Can You Really *Feel* More Confident Just By Thinking Positive Thoughts?

Well, that depends on how you *feel* when you're thinking these positive thoughts. For example, think about this sentence: *I am intelligent, and I am attractive.* While you're saying it, nod your head up and down, agree with that statement. How does that make you feel? Say it a few times until it starts to sound natural. Now, think about that same sentence again, but this time, shake your head left and right. Disagree with the statement you're thinking about. How does it make you feel? Here is another example: *I am a strong, intelligent, confident person.* When you're thinking this statement, stand up tall, throw your shoulders back, puff your chest forward, and adopt the superman pose. Say this statement repeatedly and smile when you do. How does it make you feel? Now, say the same statement, but this time slump your shoulders and hunch over, looking down like you're afraid to make eye contact. How does that make you feel?

That's the magnification effect. When you think positive thoughts and then exude the actions that back those thoughts up, your confidence levels seem to magnify. This is how those who have achieved success have been using their positive thoughts to power them along. The answer, therefore, is *yes*. You *can* make yourself feel more confident and fake it until you make it by using the appropriate actions to back up your positive, self-empowering thoughts. One of the biggest stumbling blocks in our lives is the tendency for our minds to hold onto negative thoughts. A negative mindset is easier to fall into because it requires a lot less work. Cultivating a mindset that focuses so hard on the positivity that nothing will sway it is the one that requires a lot of hard work.

But overcoming this stumbling block is the very first step you need to start building the confidence you've always hoped for. Understandably, being negative seems to come a lot easier, but if you want to start building that confident personality for yourself instead of just admiring it on others, you're going to have to change your mind, and this means slowly getting rid of negativity. Successful people always preach about one core concept, and that concept is cultivating a positive mind. To learn how to see the silver lining in the situations that you have to go through. Evaluate the people who are the closest to you, are they a positive influence, or are they negative influence. Keeping a close circle of positive people is essential to making this technique effective. This must be one of your core priorities from this point forward. To be positive, even if you don't feel like doing it, do it. Do it until it becomes second nature to you. Napoleon Hill once said if you can see it in your mind and believe in it, then you can achieve it. Visualization is such a powerful tool that, unfortunately, very often gets underestimated the same way confidence does. But did you ever stop to think that if you can visualize all the bad scenarios and things that could go wrong and believe in it so much that it manifests itself physically and is strong enough to stop you from doing something, why can't it work the other way around? If you can visualize the negative, then you can visualize the positive, and if you want to start building up the confidence to be able to small talk with any stranger, you're going to have to start focusing more on the positive visualization aspect.

You need to visualize the life that you want for yourself. You need to visualize that you're confident, happy, successful. That you're just as good as everyone else out there, and you deserve to chase after your goals the same way they did. Nothing is a bigger confidence killer than thinking someone is better than you are and wishing you were more like them. This is a common pattern that can be seen in those who suffer from low self-esteem, which is why they tend to shy away from others and beat themselves up all the time by constantly thinking they're never good enough or never going to be as good enough as someone else. *Visualize, visualize, visualize.* Spend every free moment you have pictured yourself as a confident person, a person who is interesting, and a person people want to talk to whenever you're in a room or a gathering. Picture yourself thriving in every conversation, and cement that image strongly in your mind until it starts to manifest itself into reality. Don't forget about the accompanying actions like nodding your head and standing up tall with a smile on your face to back up this mental image.

Confidence Is More Than a Need. It's A Necessity.

Being confident will shift your perspective on a lot of things, including how you view talking to people and the relationships that you form with them. When you're confident, there is no room for negativity in your life anymore, especially as your belief in yourself grows stronger over time. People naturally gravitate towards people who exude positivity and have a great outlook on life, and that will, in turn, make handling small talk sessions a much easier process for you. Confidence begins in your mind, and it is a state of mind that you and only you have the power to change. You must want to change the way you think about yourself and let go of all those negative connotations you previously associated with yourself. There are plenty of ways you can help to strengthen your mindset over time to tell yourself that you are a confident person who is more than capable of handling anything that comes your way.

Confidence is considered a soft skill, and you need both hard and soft skills in life to succeed. Once you embrace the idea that you *need* to have confidence in your life, you can begin taking the necessary steps to start building the confident mindset needed to help you get anything you want in life. Yes, you need to embrace the idea of confidence is a necessity first because this is the only way to open your mind and be receptive to the steps that must be taken. If you don't, you're going to subconsciously resist these steps, and everything is either going to feel difficult or unnatural. Open your mind to the idea that if you want to succeed, this is what you need. A shift in your mindset is the first step in the process. You need to start perceiving yourself and the world around you differently. Confidence is built through practice and relevant experience. What does relevant experience mean? It is simply building the experience that you need in the area that you want to improve your confidence in. For example, giving a speech for the 10th time is going to be a lot less nerve-wracking compared to your first time. William Jennings Bryan, the former U.S Secretary of State, once said: *"The way to develop self-*

confidence is to do the thing you fear and get a record of successful experience behind you." Basically, you need to practice standing up to what makes you nervous and uncomfortable.

It is time to create a shift in your mindset and be proud of everything you are. Be proud of your strengths and embrace your weaknesses. They both define the person that you are. A positive state of mind will always win out at the end of the day. It may require a lot more work since negativity has a stronger influence, but it always wins. Always. Even the most confident people today have to fight hard to keep negativity at bay, and that includes developing the ability to separate themselves from their weaknesses. Once you have built that foundation of strengths to focus on, it's time to identify what your weak spots are. There will be some qualities you might never be able to change, and it's okay to accept those flaws. Nobody out there is perfect, and you shouldn't put that pressure on yourself to be flawless either. Greater strength comes from the ability to accept both your flaws and your weaknesses, and once you've identified the weak spots you can improve on, focus on ways to make them better. Our brains are naturally wired for negativity, and it takes the brain four times longer to store good things than bad. We search for flaws before we focus on strengths, and we prefer to criticize before we complement them. We're instinctively drawn to negativity, and we don't treat ourselves any differently. Your confidence lies in your ability to pay attention to your talents, your strengths, your achievements, and the advantages you have to offer. Commit time each day to remind yourself of your strengths to start boosting your confidence.

What Confident People *Don't Do*

Confidence is not the same as egotistical swagger. When people believe in themselves and their abilities, they don't need to be boastful or arrogant. Confident people display certain behaviors that set them apart from everyone else, and here are some behaviors they definitely *don't* engage in:

- **They Don't Focus Too Much on Appearances** - Confident people accept themselves for the way they are. They love their bodies and the way they look, size, flaws, and all. They look after their bodies and eat healthy food because they know they deserve to be well looked after.
- **They Don't Try to Change Who They Are** - You will never catch a truly confident person trying to be someone that they are not. It doesn't matter if they are an introvert or extrovert. Confidence comes from within, and both personality types are capable of exuding confidence. They know that feeling good about who they are leads to self-assurance. They know they can achieve so much more if they stay authentic and remain true to who they are. They learned long ago that self-acceptance is a vital part of

becoming a confident person, that is why you'll never see them trying to be someone else or being fake just to fit in.

- **They Don't Compare -** Put a stop to the comparison, and you'll find that you're much happier when you do. There is no point in comparing yourself to someone else because the truth is, you're never going to be that person. You're as unique as your thumbprint is. No two people are alike; the same way no two sets of thumbprints will ever be alike. It's how we distinguish ourselves from the rest. Comparison is a destructive habit, and it will do nothing to help the successful mindset you're trying to build. You're unique, and you have the potential to reach your own kind of success. To become more confident, that pernicious voice in your mind must be silenced.
- **They Don't Crave Likes and Follows on Social Media -** If someone likes something they've shared, great! If they don't, that's okay too. A confident person is not bothered by superficial likes and follows on social media. Confident people don't need social media to feel good about themselves. They don't need social media to validate that they are awesome. To the confident person, social media is merely an entertaining place to share content and maybe catch up with what other people are doing. Their profiles are usually filled with interesting content since they tend to be less self-centered than those who are on social media fishing for compliments.
- **They Don't Think Other People Know Best -** They never assume that other people always know better than they do. Confident people trust their own judgment and never look to others for validation or approval. They value their opinions and listen to their own intuition. They trust that they know what is in their best interest, and they are confident enough to carry out actions even if others disagree with them. They may seek guidance or input from trusted sources, but they end up making the final decision when the time comes.
- **They Don't Wait for Anyone's Permission -** A confident person will never need someone else to tell them what to do all the time. The only time the confident person asks a lot of questions or looks to others is when they are new at something or trying to familiarize themselves with a routine or a new situation. They rarely ever wait to be told what to do. They see what needs to be done, and they are confident enough in their abilities to get the job done.
- **They Never Put Someone Else Down -** Confident people don't feel the need to put other people down to make themselves feel good. They're not afraid of competition. In fact, they welcome it and use the competition as motivation to do even better. They

don't feel the need to undermine others, and this is something you'll never find them doing. If they do notice that certain toxic people around them are indulging in this kind of behavior, they move away from that. When someone else succeeds, they are genuinely happy for those people. Rather than resent someone else's success, the confident person uses that as motivation for themselves to do better.

- **They Don't Try to Dominate Conversations** - Confident people treat conversations like an exchange of healthy ideas and thoughts. They don't try to dominate a conversation just to prove they are more interesting, or that they know better. They don't mind doing the listening if it means they get to learn a little bit about what someone else is passionate about.
- **They Don't Actively Try and Avoid Conflict** - Confident people understand that conflict is a part of life. You're not always going to get along with everyone around you. Once in a while, heads will butt, and they are confident enough to stand up for themselves if they feel the need to. For the confident person, conflict is something that can be managed effectively, and thus, they don't try to run away from it, live in denial, or try to people-please their way through life in the hopes of avoiding conflict.
- **They Don't Cling to Others** - You'll never find a confident person who is needy and desperate. It goes with the territory of being comfortable enough in their own skin that they don't fear being alone sometimes. They do enjoy the company of others, but at the same time, they're comfortable enough to enjoy their own company.
- **They Don't Depend on External Elements for Happiness** - They don't rely on social media for happiness. They don't depend on the approval and acceptance of others for happiness. Happiness is a very *critical* element of confidence. To be happy with what you do, you need to be happy with who you are. Those who are brimming with confidence derive pleasure from the sense of satisfaction they get from a job well done. They know happiness comes from within, and no matter what anyone else may think, they understand you are never as good or bad as people say you are. That is true confidence.

CHAPTER 2
Moving Out Of Your Comfort Zone

Would you believe it if you were told that the more you subjected yourself to discomfort, the *happier* you will be? Think about all those times you had to step out of your comfort zone. Yes, it was uncomfortable. Yes, you felt like quitting and giving up. You might have even questioned several times, *"Why am I doing this?."* The problem is, not everyone is willing to regularly push themselves to step out of their comfort zones. Especially if you lack confidence in yourself and your abilities.

What Is a Comfort Zone?

A comfort zone is actually a psychological state of mind. It happens when you're comfortable and familiar with your surroundings and your routine. You will know you're in your comfort zone when you feel at ease, and you feel like you are in control of your environment. In their comfort zones, most people experience lower levels of stress and anxiety because, well, they have some sense of control over themselves and their current environment. Is it possible to still perform when you're in your comfort zone? Yes, it is, but your performance is only going to be steady or stagnated. That is because you're working at a certain pace that you're already comfortable and familiar with, which means you're probably not pushing yourself harder the way you could be.

Author Judith M. Bardwick explains in her book, *The Dangers Of the Comfort Zone,* that this zone is typically where a person can operate from an anxiety-neutral position. University of Houston Graduate College of Social Work research professor, Brene Brown, describes the comfort zone as a place where vulnerability, uncertainty, and scarcity are at minimal levels. When we feel we have some semblance of control, we're content and comfortable. Hence the term comfort zone.

The idea of stepping *outside* of these zones and into uncertainty where we can't control what might happen causes anxiety for many people. If we're already comfortable in a certain way, why bother trying to change that? The problem with getting too comfortable in your comfort zone is, you end up not wanting to get out of that zone. Why would you when it's just so comfortable? A lack of confidence would just aggravate the situation even more, because when we become too complacent with the way things are, subconsciously we start to seek out reasons and excuses to avoid any kind of responsibility that would push us out of that comfort zone. We love to do what we're comfortable with, and this is why we find it so hard to venture outside our comfort zone. We love familiarity, and we're resistant to change because it makes it uncomfortable. Comfort zones keep you safe from the possibility of failure, judgment, criticism, stress, and all those unpleasant feelings you have to go through before you reach the peak of your success. These are all valid concerns too. No wonder it is such a struggle to decide to leave this zone. Even more so when you're not confident that you can achieve a successful outcome if you do make that choice.

But This Is a Dangerous Zone to Be In

We don't want to admit it, but we love what is familiar and comfortable. Going back to old habits and familiar patterns seem like a better option instead of having to deal with the unknown. An unknown where there is a real possibility you might fail or risk not being good enough. Change creates a new awareness, new perspective, poses a huge threat to what has been so comfortable and familiar. Even if what was once so comfortable and familiar is no longer satisfying or fulfilling. No matter which way you turn, you're faced with the prospect of destroying what you have just learned you want or destroying who you have been now that you've learned you want to become someone new. As if that wasn't bad enough, with all the stress coming from the prospect of change, you've now ignited the stress response in your body that creates a cascade of stress-related illnesses or symptoms. It becomes so much easier to self-sabotage than you have to deal with all this pressure. It becomes so much easier to decide to stay in your comfort zone.

Comfort zones keep you stuck where you are, but at the same time, they keep you safe. Your head is spinning with all sorts of questions about how change is going to impact your life, what relationships might be lost along the way, what you would need to sacrifice. It all becomes too much to deal with at some point. Some people are so resistant to change, and they're terrified of it to the point where they self-sabotage. We self-sabotage because we don't like it when something is too risky or uncertain. If given the choice, we would all prefer to stay in our comfort zones. Self-sabotage is what happens when you're approaching the edge of that comfort zone or when you've passed that comfort zone line.

What makes the comfort zone so dangerous is that your mind starts to convince you that the struggle is not worth it, and you start doing things that don't allow you to overcome the challenges you face. The changes you know you'll have to face could create such a snowball domino effect. You begin to do anything you can to protect yourself from feeling that kind of anxiety. Success is hard work. Overcoming challenges is hard work. Change to achieve success is great, but at the same time, it could impact so much you're afraid of what is to come. There's a mental or subconscious part of you that tells you to backtrack or give up when something becomes too hard. Having to evict the zone that you feel comfortable in is not an easy pill to swallow. You will be tested, pushed to your limits; at times, you may cry and feel like you want to give up. It's hard to see it when it is happening, but every challenge that you face from the moment you leave your comfort zone is making you stronger. Every challenge is designed to make you a better person if you can see it through to the end.

No matter how good that zone may feel, what makes you comfortable is going to ruin you. You *need* to encounter hardship to grow as a person. Only in a state of discomfort can we continue to grow. The environment that you live in is going to dictate whether you grow or remain stuck where you are. Your environment is going to either promote your growth or hinder it. Think of a goldfish that lives in a fishbowl. The environment that the goldfish lives in will dictate its size. In a fishbowl, it is safe, but it usually doesn't grow very big because the size of the fishbowl is hindering its growth. If that goldfish was placed in a bigger and wider environment, like a pond, for example, there's more room for growth. However, it also faces the danger of being eaten by bigger fish in that environment, so the goldfish has a reason to grow bigger in size to give itself a fighting chance. Your environment is like that proverbial fishbowl. Stay in your comfort zone, and like the goldfish, there is only so much you can grow. But broadening your horizons and the risks that you face will be a motivating factor for you to become stronger than ever to give yourself a fighting chance.

Think of your current environments where you live, work, and play. All of these are proverbial fish bowls that are dictating your current growth. When you live in a state of stagnation in your comfort zone, your creativity and independent thought are stifled. This is why you don't grow much in this zone, and your performance can only go so far. Comfort zones are low-performing growth zones. You need to train your mind to believe you have what it takes to succeed. You might believe that you have a desire to succeed in a certain path, but subconsciously in the back of your mind, you don't believe that you have what it takes to make it happen. If you don't believe you deserve it, you're always going to self-sabotage, even when you think you're not doing it. Life begins when you burst through your comfort zone, and the only way to do that is to get rid of all those self-sabotaging habits that have been holding you back all along. Pushing beyond your comfort zone is like a muscle you work during exercise. It's hard at first, but the more you do it, the easier it starts to become. If you've ever procrastinated, made excuses, lacked clarity suddenly, and even doubt your own greatness, then you need to pay attention.

We Know We Need to Change, So Why Are We Still Hesitating?

Because of the chaos, you're afraid to confront. When you don't have control over what happens around you, it feels like your world is descending into chaos. When your environment is not in order, it is not desirable. When there is no predictability, we become afraid. We're afraid when the outcome is not guaranteed, and we're afraid of what is going to happen to us should we fall flat on our faces. We know being comfortable is dangerous because it means we're not growing as a person. Yet, it feels like a struggle to put one foot in front of the other, pushing yourself out of your comfort zone anyway because, well, we're afraid. *Growth can only happen in a state of discomfort.* Let this be the mantra that pushes you forward.

Yes, you may not feel very confident right now, but there is going to be *zero* chance that you are ever going to become the confident person you hope to be if you continue to stay in your comfort zone. Confidence cannot be developed if you're not moving anywhere. If we think about it, it is not the challenges that we are afraid of most of the time. It is the *unpredictability* and the lack of control that those challenges bring. Not having an outcome that is certain or expected can lead to a lot of "what if" questions. Those questions terrify us because the answers and speculations we make only feed into any existing negative thoughts we might have.

Actively seeking discomfort to become a better, stronger, and more confident person might not be something you want to hear. But it is something you *must-do* if you hope to change for the better. Outside your comfort zone is the only real place that success can be achieved. It is the only place where a greater sense of self-confidence and self-esteem can be developed. Beyond the walls of your comfort zone lie a whole realm of possibilities. The opportunities out there are yours for the taking. But all of this and more cannot happen if you continue to allow yourself to remain *stuck*.

Stepping Out of Your Comfort Zone Can Be a Good Thing

When we have to venture into the unfamiliar, our stress response is triggered. This can be a good thing since it also enhances our level of focus on concentration since our brain is telling us we need to be alert. Believe it or not, your performance can actually be *enhanced* when there's a certain amount of stress introduced into the mix. As uncomfortable as change might be, it's important to consistently remind yourself that change can be a good thing if you let it. Stress is the way our bodies react to the stimuli that it is exposed to. Generally, stress is experienced as a short-term reaction, and it usually goes away, and our bodies return to normal once the cause of the stress has passed. Depending on the way you handle it and how it affects you, stress can either be a good thing or a bad thing. Good stress kicks in to help you pull those long all-nighters to meet important deadlines and push past your boundaries to see what you're capable of. Bad stress, however, leaves you with insomnia, a lack of clarity, and the constant feeling of being on edge like your last nerve is about to snap at any minute.

Sometimes, we voluntarily choose to step out of our comfort zones. Other times, we may be forced into it. Like when our employer suddenly has to let us go because of an economic downturn. When you're forced to leave your comfort zone with no other choice, the way you respond will dictate how much you grow and how much confidence you develop along the way. Other times, we may be encouraged out of our comfort zones by other people who push us to be better. That is one form of good stress. Good stress is the adrenaline rush you need to help you overcome the challenges you face so you can cross the finish line of every goal you set for yourself. Small amounts of good stress keep us challenged, motivated, interested, and continuously striving to do better. To be better. Chaos is good for development. Comfort zones stifle your development.

Breaking Out of Your Comfort Zone Killers

What needs to happen now is that our minds must be retrained. We need to rewire our minds to relish in discomfort. How? By reminding ourselves that these discomforts never last. Like a storm, it comes, and it goes. All we need to do is be strong enough to weather that storm. Before you begin working on building your confidence, the skill that you need to develop first is the skill that helps you break out of your comfort zone. Let's talk about some of the common comfort zone killers and how you can break out of them:

- **You're Letting Fear Keep You In the Zone** - Fear is the biggest comfort zone killer. When we're afraid to face our fears, we tend to rationalize and find reasons *not* to do something. The only way to break out of this comfort zone killer is to acknowledge your fear, but then push yourself to do it anyway. Face up to your fears, no matter how terrified it makes you. Do it one step at the time, put one foot in front of the other. You don't have to dive headfirst of the deep end when you're afraid. It is okay to take your time as long as you keep moving forward. What we need to realize is that there is no running away from our fears. Even though it is the easier thing to do, you cannot spend the rest of your life running away from your obstacles. You've only got one short, precious life to live, and if you waste it all by running all the time, you're going to reach your retirement years and look back filled with regret. The most persistent people are the ones more likely to achieve success because they have the discipline and the drive to never give up and always keep moving forward. This is because they are engaged in habits that work for them, and they have diligently trained themselves to have the discipline to stick to these habits. If you want to stop self-sabotage, you need to be persistent and to stop running away from the things that you're afraid of. The self-sabotaging thought will come creeping into your mind, enticing you to give up each time you struggle, but you need to train your mind to be stronger than the thoughts that you have. What we need to realize is that the longer we hesitate and rationalize why we shouldn't do something, the harder it is going to be to face up to your fears. You have to steel yourself and push back against it by doing the hard thing and keep moving forward. Like ripping off a bandaid, do it in one swift, quick motion. No matter what you feel like or what your mind is telling you to do, keep pushing forward.

- **Not Being Focused Enough On Your Goals** - Another comfort zone killer that stops us from moving forward. When you're not focused enough on your goals, you become easily distracted. When you're easily distracted, you lose focus. When you lose focus, it's easy to talk yourself out of not doing something, and the excuses come pouring in. You need to identify what your current behavior patterns are that prevent you from staying focused on your goals. Next, think about what you can do to rectify those patterns. What you need to do is reflect on your daily behavior. Think about this for a minute. Where are you guilty of slowing down when you know you should be speeding up? Reflect on some of the things you've done in the past too. What you're trying to identify are the ways that you've self-sabotaged in the past. What lies outside your comfort zone may feel weird, but you need to remember that challenge only means you're doing something to better yourself. Positive change cannot take place if you choose to stay where you are and never move. Identify when you're feeling resistant when you've pushed a little outside your comfort zone, and then think about what you can do to help you overcome that resistance.

- **Be Willing to Try Something New** - The idea of something new can be both scary and exciting at the same time. It depends entirely on how you choose to look at it. You see, most of the time, we are not willing to try something new because of the limiting beliefs we carry with us. We *think* we're not good enough, not talented enough, not passionate enough, not equipped enough, and we could come up with a whole bunch of other reasons why. But we will never know what the outcome really is unless we *try*. Toss out the limiting beliefs that are holding you back because these only keep you in your comfort zone. If you're afraid of starting your own business, ask yourself why? What's the reason behind that fear? What is that self-limiting belief that is holding you back, and is it justified? Why are you afraid of getting into a serious relationship? What limiting beliefs are holding you back from the belief that the relationship can be happy and fulfilling? Reframe your mindset because you need to believe that you're worthy; otherwise, no matter how hard you work, you're always going to find some obstacle or other blocking you. Part of your new mindset for success needs to be a new belief. A belief that you deserve all that you desire. Believe that you have what it takes to make your dreams come true. Without the confidence and belief in your own self-worth, you will always find it a challenge to value yourself, love yourself, or even name any positive traits that you may have. You don't have to lose something immediately to get started breaking out of your comfort zone. All you have to do is adopt a willing attitude to try and be open to seeing how it plays out.

- **You're Striving for Perfection** - How often have you told yourself you would be willing to do something *"if only"* it was a certain way. That you would have been willing to do something if X or Y had been in your favor. Striving for perfectionism is striving for a concept that does not exist. You can never be 100% perfect because no one can. Life simply does not work that way, and we're only human, this means that yes, we do make mistakes from time to time. Holding on to this comfort zone killer is only going to keep you trapped, never moving forward because you're striving for something that does not exist. Novelist and writer Anne Lamott eloquently put it when she said: *Perfectionism is the voice of the oppressor, and it is the enemy of people.* Perfectionism is not all bad, but if you're an over-thinker, this is one habit you need to rid yourself of because of the constant pressure you face to meet unrealistic standards. If you want to break out of your comfort zone, let go of this concept that you need things to be a certain, perfect way before you can move forward. Overthinkers are guilty of using this as an excuse not to budge from their comfort zone. They don't trust their judgment, and they are not confident in their abilities. One part of that is because they struggle with perfectionism that is unrealistic. When they fall short, they feel incompetent and lose confidence in their abilities. Self- doubt can be a crippling burden to bear, and as soon it gets a foothold in your mind, it can be a very tough habit to break out of. We know that we shouldn't focus on the negative. We know we should believe in ourselves. *Perfectionism does not exist.* You worry so much about everything that could go wrong, and you try to overcompensate by attempting to control nearly everything around them to the point of perfectionism. While perfectionism may sound like a good thing, it isn't because it is simply not possible to be perfect all the time. When you fail to gain the control you want, it only makes the negative the limiting beliefs you're telling yourself seem much worse. Let go of perfectionism and instead, just try your best at everything you do.

The Fundamental Steps to Start With

Everybody is afraid of something. Even successful people are afraid of something. We're all afraid of something, and this knowledge can liberate you from putting so much pressure on yourself to be perfect all the time. It can free you from the pressure of thinking you need to be a "certain way" before you can begin taking the steps you need to improve yourself. Your journey to greater confidence begins at the end of your comfort zone. It takes *courage* to do the things that you are afraid of, and this is what you're going to take away from this chapter. The courage to break free of your limiting beliefs. The courage to face the fear of the unknown and what you cannot control. When courage is combined with confidence, you become *unstoppable*. Before you can get to confidence, though, you're going to need to take steps to break out of your comfort zone.

As Winston Churchill once said: *"Courage is rightly considered the foremost of all virtues, for, upon it, all others depend."* The braver you become with each fear you overcome, the more confident you subsequently become too. Don't become one of those people who are so afraid to dream big that they shut themselves down even before they have had a chance to get started. NO, you need to believe that anything is possible if you want it badly enough. To break out of this very limiting bubble of comfort you're living in, this is what you need to do:

- **Commit Wholeheartedly** - It doesn't matter what you're thinking about doing. Commit to it wholeheartedly. Focus entirely on doing it and finishing it. Everything else is secondary. The possibilities of what might happen and the speculations you make are secondary. All successful people achieve victory because they are fully committed and engaged in the task they decide to take on. The phrase "throw yourself entirely into your work" is how you stay focused. Committing completely and wholeheartedly is how you stop yourself from being sidetracked by your fears. Our minds can be resistant to change when it's taking us out of our comfort zone. Life is not always going to go according to plan, and the more willing and prepared you are to adapt and change to the circumstances, the easier it will be for your brain to switch back into the focus mode it needs. It's okay if you don't have a guarantee. All you need to do to overcome your current challenge is to be involved wholeheartedly in your activities. If you fail, at least you know you failed while you were trying your best, and there is always next time to try again. Remember, it took Edison 1,000 tries before he found the lightbulb. If he can try 1,000 times without ever giving up, you can do it too.

- **Have the Courage to Move Into the Discomfort Zone -** The zone where awkwardness and discomfort sometimes rule the day. The zone where fear and anxieties lead the charge because our fears allow them to be set free. In your quest for success, there is no enemy greater than that of your comfort zone, and the only way to overcome this is to be willing to move into the other zone. The zone that nobody wants to find themselves in. The *discomfort zone*. The thing we need to remember is that the life of our dreams doesn't happen when we're stuck in a rut. It happens when we have the courage we need to relocate. Having the courage to move with only faith on your side and no guarantee of success seems like a lot to ask.
- **Repeatedly Do What You're Afraid Of -** One way of working through your fears is to face it repeatedly until you no longer feel afraid. As you begin preparing to breach your comfort zone boundaries, pick one fear to work on, and focus on overcoming that fear first before you move onto the next fear. For example, if you're afraid of public speaking and giving speeches because you're not feeling confident on stage yet, the only way to get through it is to repeatedly force yourself to give speeches until you're no longer afraid of the stage and the audience anymore. It could take you 10 speeches before you reach this level. Maybe even 20 speeches. But the one thing you will notice is that the minute the fear is gone, it is replaced by confidence. This confidence is only going to grow with each speech you make. Once you feel you have overcome this fear and you're not afraid anymore. It might go against your natural instinct, but you need to start running towards the things you fear. Not away from it. Dominate your fears, and you will feel like a superhero. Try it.
- **Become Your Own Validation -** You don't need anyone else to validate that you're good enough or capable enough. The only validation you need is from yourself because you are the one going through your challenges. No one else is. They will be there as support systems, but this is your solo journey to take. If you base your self-worth on whether other people approve of you or like you, you're going to struggle to break out of your comfort zone forever. If your confidence is based purely on external forces, it's not a firm foothold for you to stand on. The best way to start building your internal validation is to focus and build upon what makes you feel good. When you feel good, then you don't need others to make you feel good. Do activities that make you feel happy, surround yourself with people who make you feel awesome without having to do any favors for them. Focus on your strengths and all your best qualities and block out everything else.

You already have a lot going for you; you just need to be reminded of it.
- **Stay Focused on Solutions** - Instead of focusing on how afraid you are, how anxious you feel, or how everything is going to possibly go wrong, stay focused on solutions instead. Stay focused on the solution and block out all other distractions. At every step of the way during your thought process, ask if this is leading you towards a solution. If it's not, then change your train of thought, so you're always focused on finding a solution. The choice is yours to make, and you can choose to ask, *"What do I do from here? What is the next step? How do I overcome this? What options do I have?."* The choice always resides with you, and this is where you have the power. If you're someone who needs to have some sense of control in your life, this is where you can direct your focus towards. You are in control of the solutions you choose to go with.

The final thing you can do to build your confidence and hold onto this confidence when you're breaking out of your comfort zone is to have the courage to persist longer than anyone else. Persistence is one of the few qualities that will ultimately guarantee you succeed as what you're trying to do. When everyone else gives up and quits, you keep going. That is what confidence can do for you, and the more you practice the steps in this chapter, your confidence is only going to grow from this point onwards. You have nothing to fear and everything to gain if you learn to view every failure as a learning experience.

CHAPTER 3
Dealing With Nervous Anxiety

Sweaty palms. Heart palpitations. Nervous nail-biting. Nervous pacing back and forth. These are all indicators that you might be an anxious person. You're probably already familiar with these symptoms, especially when you're faced with the prospect of being in a social situation. When you're anxious, confidence seems like an elusive concept, depending on the severity of your condition. Anxiety can range from mild to nervous. Our bodies have a strange way of reacting when we're anxious, but the one thing that you can be sure of is that you will not be acting in a confident manner.

The problem with anxiety is that it is not a rational thing. We can't just "get over it" and "be confident," even though that is the advice most people would tell you since they don't fully understand what anxiety entails. To them, the solution is simple. Just push aside your fears, snap out of it, and be confident. Easy, right? *Not if you're an anxious person.* It's hard to remain calm, let alone think about being confident when you're fraught with nervousness. Those "you-can-do-it!" motivation type blogs and articles don't seem to help either. Those articles are trying to make you feel good about yourself again, but they're not helping because they lack any actionable or practical advice on how to tackle the root of the problem you're facing, which is your nervous anxiety. The mind can be a very powerful thing, and when it's anxious, it seems to be even more powerful than ever. Trying to put it on pause for even two seconds can require monumental effort and concentration, none of which you have when your mind and heart seems to be racing a mile a minute.

Understanding Anxiety

Originally, anxiety is a survival mechanism present in all of us. Its primary function is to alert us to the presence of danger, and it is not meant to be an emotion that lingers for long. Once the danger has passed, anxiety should dissipate, but that's not the case if you happen to be dealing with an anxiety disorder. With an anxiety disorder, the body remains in an unnatural heightened state of alertness. Everything feels like a cause for alarm, and it triggers a constant flow of cortisol throughout the body. There's no exact reason why you might be feeling nervous or anxious, either. Anxiety has no logical source, making it difficult to pinpoint what the underlying cause may be. It can be difficult to talk yourself out of an anxious episode.

Anxiety is diagnosed as a psychiatric or mental health disorder that is capable of derailing your daily life because of the persistent fear and worry that seems to follow you everywhere you go. In today's society, it is unfortunate that anxiety is not talked about enough the way it should be. This is partly due to the stigma associated with it because it is classified as a mental health issue. It is not uncommon for those struggling with anxiety to be misunderstood, even by those who are closest to them. Anxiety can be a very lonely and isolating burden to bear when you feel disconnected to the people closest to you. A lot of people who struggle with anxiety are often embarrassed to admit what they're going through because they fear being rejected.

It's hard to describe what anxiety feels like, but the closest description would be anxiety makes you feel like you're running in a hamster wheel, going round and round in circles with no productive solution or end in sight. Your days and nights seem to be filled with persistent worries that won't seem to go away, no matter how hard the person may try to reason with themselves. The fear felt can sometimes be so great that it leads to a panic attack episode. There seems to be a persistent sense of foreboding or dread like something bad is going to happen at any time. When you're anxious, your body remains in an unnatural heightened state of alertness. Everything feels like a cause for alarm, and it triggers a constant flow of cortisol throughout the body. No wonder you find it such a struggle to remain confident. It's not an easy thing to do when you've got a lot going on.

What Happens to Our Bodies When We're Anxious

Ice cold hands and feet is one symptom of extreme anxiety. That is because when you're anxious, your blood flow is all channeled toward your larger organs. This makes it hard for your blood to circulate properly throughout your body, and that is why you could look pale and feel ice-cold even when it's hot outside. Your body is going into its fight or flight mode to help you survive. When you're anxious, you could also be prone to eating and drinking more quickly, which could lead to excessive gas in your body. You might find that you need to go to the toilet a lot more frequently too because the muscles tensing up in your body are going to put some pressure on some of your internal organs. Like your bladder, for example. Muscle tension is a common side effect of nervous anxiety. Anxious individuals, like those with Generalized Anxiety Disorder, find that they tend to breathe more rapidly than other people do. When you breathe rapidly, your brain is tricked into thinking that you need more oxygen. This will cause you to take deep breaths, and sometimes, you end up yawning a lot to try and get more oxygen flow to the brain. Have you got an uncomfortable itch? Anxiety could be behind that too. Because you're anxious, it could make you more prone to a lot of skin allergies and problems like developing a rash when you're extremely stressed. That's the extra cortisol churning through your body. When all those hormones are rushing through your veins, your skin starts to feel irritated.

Do you find that you have difficulty concentrating? Well, that could be because of your anxiety too. Sometimes it feels like you're having an out of body experience, especially when things start to feel too overwhelming. Everything starts to feel surreal, and there is a reason for this. It is because your body is going through what is known as the fight or flight response. Oh, and frequent headaches and migraines could also be a potential side effect of this condition. The tension and the pressure brought on by staying in a period of prolonged negativity is like putting a tight rubber band around your head, constricting it. This can cause a lot of pressure and discomfort, and you might feel like your head is about to explode at times when you're so overwhelmed by your thoughts. Headaches and migraines are a common symptom among those who struggle with excessive thoughts that also happen to trigger their anxiety.

When you're stressed out all the time, you're not a confident person. Instead, what you become is an irritable, impatient, and sometimes angry person. Being in a stressed-out state all the time will leave anyone feeling on edge, and this happens a lot when you're anxious. They become easily irritable, snapping at the slightest provocation because they're already a big bundle of tense nerves, to begin with. If you find yourself easily irritable, angry, or emotional at the drop of a hat, the chances are you're overwhelmed by your emotions and probably feeling anxious thanks to all the excessive thoughts running wild in your head.

To Fight or Take Flight?

This response is the reason behind the out of body experience you sometimes go through when you're feeling extremely anxious. It is your body's way of coping by removing the excess stimuli that it thinks is too much for you to handle. Our fight-or-flight response is a reaction to stress, and this is a reaction that most likely evolved out of the survival needs from our early ancestors who lived in dangerous times. Our early cavemen ancestors were in constant danger of animals. One minute they might be lighting a fire, and the next minute, there's a stampede coming their way, and they need to evacuate as soon as possible. The human body's natural survival design then kicks in, and we have a full surge of energy and strength to quickly respond to the threat by removing ourselves from danger and increasing our chances of survival. Even though it is a survival mechanism, your body is not meant to remain in this state of alertness for long. All that cortisol pumping through your body will eventually take its toll on your mental, physical, and emotional health.

Am I An Introvert? Or Is It Anxiety?

An introvert is someone who prefers their own company. When you're an introvert, you consider yourself someone who is reserved and quiet. There is nothing wrong with being an introvert. Not in the least, since it takes all sorts of personalities to create this beautiful, diverse world we live in. Imagine if we lived in a world where everyone was an extrovert? There wouldn't be any balance, and it would be hard to find time for yourself if people always love to talk, talk, talk. But even introverts can be confident when they need to rise to the occasion. This is not the case when someone is dealing with social anxiety.

If it is anxiety or social anxiety (the more serious variant) that you're dealing with, you have an intense fear of social situations. The very idea of being around people, particularly people you don't know, *terrifies you*. It makes you so anxious that, depending on your fear level, you could induce a panic attack and start hyperventilating at the very thought of social situations. Social anxiety is a disorder, and the official acronym for it is *SAD (Social Anxiety Disorder)*. SAD can manifest in several ways, from shyness and nervousness to dreading everyday activities because it means you need to be around people. Whenever you know you have to go out in public, you start sweating and feeling nervous, like your heart is racing a mile a minute. These anxious heart palpitations can make it feel like it's hard to breathe sometimes.

The problem with SAD is that, like anxiety in general, it can be attributed to a number of factors. An even bigger problem is the way that it can affect your physical and mental health, and of course, your confidence along with it. It's hard to feel like a confident person when nervous beads of sweat keep dripping off your forehead, and you feel like you can't stop shaking and trembling. SAD could be caused by the way your brain is genetically structured, a traumatic event you went through in life, your environment and upbringing, the list could keep going. Let's take a closer look at the difference between someone who is an introvert and someone who struggles with SAD:

An introvert is:
- A person who is focused on themselves and their mental state of health.
- Usually perceived as someone who tends to focus inwards and look within themselves to find the answers they seek.
- A person who likes to spend time alone because they feel like it helps them recharge their batteries.
- A person who prefers their own company. They would prefer to be at home curled up with a good book rather than be out partying with a group of strangers.
- A person who actively seeks solitude to reconnect with themselves. In fact, they find these moments of solitude rewarding.

- Someone who is not against being social, but they are particular about who they would prefer to spend their time with.
- A person who enjoys doing things by themselves in the comfort of their own home.
- A person who is selective about the circle of friends and people they choose to keep close to them. They usually have a few good people in their life with whom they share a strong bond.

An anxious person is:
- A person who is frightened of social events to the point that they sometimes turn down invitations because they can't deal with the stress. It is not that they would rather be at home, but they're paralyzed by their fears.
- A person who feels uneasy at the thought of being around people. They might get nervous butterflies in their stomach or feel queasy and lightheaded from all that stress.
- A person who doesn't like being out in social situations because they are always worried about how others are perceiving them. They worry if people are talking about them behind their backs. They worry if people think poorly of them.
- A person who feels dread when things are not in their control. This explains why they hate social events. They can't control how the event is going to go, how their interactions with other people are going to go, and they can't control the outcome of what might happen at those events. This makes them extremely nervous, and they feel vulnerable and exposed.
- A person who struggles a lot internally since they can't make their fears known to anyone. They're too afraid of being perceived as weird, and the truth is, not everyone is going to understand what it is like to live with anxiety all the time.
- A person who might have become so reclusive that they don't go out and do things anymore unless they are left with no other option.
- A person who becomes distressed when they find themselves being in a situation where they are the center of attention. They become distressed when they feel they are being watched or observed while they are doing something.
- A person who becomes distressed when they feel insecure and out of place in social situations, very often uttering the phrase I don't really know what to say.
- A person who feels distressed and constantly wants to withdraw from the limelight to avoid any unwanted attention.
- A person who doesn't enjoy the activities that they used to anymore because every social event feels daunting.
- A person who struggles to maintain relationships.

- A person who becomes distressed, nervous, and visibly awkward and uncomfortable when being introduced to new people.

For those struggling with anxiety, confidence is almost nonexistent. They can leave messages unread for days, emails unanswered, phone calls not returned for no specific reason. Most of the time, they try to avoid any possibility of conflict, and if their anxiety is bad enough, they leave messages unanswered for days simply because they are worried the conversation could be a bad one. When you're dealing with anxiety or its more severe form, SAD, you find yourself experiencing feelings of fear, apprehension, and nervousness, often prominent when you think that you might be put in a social situation in which you could possibly do something humiliating and embarrassing. For example, if you had to enter a room in which everyone is already seated down, and they are the last one to arrive, you fear that you could possibly trip and fall over and even worse, everyone in the entire room will take notice and laugh at them, a thought which is completely mortifying.

Dealing with nervous anxiety is not fun. Dealing with SAD is not fun either. How do you become a confident person when you're struggling to remain calm in the presence of others? How do you become a confident person when you dread the thought of being around people? SAD can eventually lead to loneliness and isolation because of the constant avoidance of human interaction. Those who live with SAD don't necessarily experience these feelings only when they are thrust into a new environment or situation. Sometimes the symptoms can even manifest themselves in familiar situations too, even around family and friends whom you are familiar with. Certain types of anxiety, like SAD, can be a chronic disorder, to a point where even everyday interactions cause extreme amounts of anxiety, fear, self-consciousness, and embarrassment because you fear being judged and scrutinized by others, even though they aren't necessarily doing it. SAD, in its chronic form, can result in it disrupting your daily routine, work, school, and any other activities because you feel like you can't cope well enough to perform those activities.

It's hard to be a confident person when anxiety turns you into someone who is in constant need of reassurance all the time. Anxiety sufferers don't seek out praise and recognition. When you're dealing with anxiety, you'll seek out reassurance to the point you might become obsessed with it. Anxiety sufferers continually seek validation and approval, wondering if what they did was good enough. Did I do this okay? Was this good? Did I mess up? Did I say or do something that might have offended someone? Was it okay to do that? Was it okay to say that? That's not the mark of someone who is confident. Not even a little bit. Anxiety will make you the opposite of what a confident person should be. You find it hard to trust your own judgment, and you're always double-checking and wondering, seeking reassurance that you're okay. You'll get stuck in your, unable to move onto the next task until you get the recognition you need to feel better about yourself.

Calming the Mind, Body, and Soul

When anxiety strikes, it is best not to think about being confident just yet. Instead, focus on calming your mind, body, and soul first before you attempt to do anything else. Those who deal with anxiety tend to have increased or heightened levels of arousal where their body is tense and on edge because of the stress hormones pumping through their veins at the time. Your mind and body are already going through a lot when you have to deal with something like this, and confidence is going to be the last thing on your mind. You need to try and take some deep breaths and do your best to calm your mind and body down. Understandably, this seems impossible unless you've got the right coping strategies to help you do it. What you need to do is arm yourself with one or two of the strategies from the list below and use them as your go-to options whenever anxiety rises within you.

A muscle relaxation technique that works really well when you're feeling nervous or anxious is called the *Progressive Muscle Relaxation Technique*. Using this technique, you would focus on taking deep breaths in and out. Each time you exhale, focus on releasing one muscle area of your body. Start by breathing in deeply, and on the exhale, loosen the muscle in your shoulder area as the air flows out of your body. Take another deep breath in, and on the exhale, relax your arms right down to your fingers. Repeat the process and go through all the areas of your body where you feel tense, progressively relaxing your muscles along the way. Once you've slowed down your racing mind, the next step is to regulate your emotions. This can be accomplished through mindfulness. Pay attention to the thoughts that run through your mind and the way your body is responding to them. That's the first step in taking control. Instead of letting the emotions go wild and unruly, pause and mindfully reflect on how you feel the impact it has on you. If your stress is making your shoulders hurt, take a few deep breaths and mindfully allow your body to relax.

How to Be Confident Even If You're Dealing with Anxiety

Depending on the severity of the anxiety you experience, there are ways you can work around your nervousness to appear confident, even if you might not be feeling 100% confident as yet. The trick is to give your mind something else to focus on besides how nervous you feel. Contrary to what you might think, you don't need as much confidence as you think. You can still *appear* to be confident even if the butterflies in your stomach are flapping their wings rapidly. If you give your mind something else to focus on, you can change the way that you think about your fears. Let's look at this example to illustrate that point. Imagine you are faced with a new challenge. You need to meet someone new, and this usually generates a lot of worry, fear, and anxiety for you. You worry that you might run out of things to say. You're worried you might not have anything in common to talk about. You're worried there might be too many awkward pauses in the conversation that make both you and the other person nervous. The anxious mind has a lot of worries that it could latch on to, and it does this because there is nothing else to focus on. No anchor point that it can use to steady itself.

In your mind, you are not brave enough to meet that new person for the first time. You think there is too much pressure involved, and you're worried you can't do it. Your anxiety will get the best of you unless you start shifting the way that you think. For example, you don't need to worry about the *entire* conversation all at once. All you need to focus on is the very start of the conversation; the part where you introduce yourself with a firm handshake, and a smile on your face. For any challenge, getting started is always the hardest part. But once you have got over this initial hump, everything quickly moves along. If you can muster up enough courage to take the first step and overcome that first big obstacle, then you know that you can handle anything that follows after that.

If you don't feel confident enough yet to face your social anxieties, there is nothing to worry about. Like everything else in this process, building that confidence is going to take time and practice. Practice makes perfect, and the following strategies are going to help you work on your confidence while still giving the impression that you are, well, not nervous at all:

- **Don't Make It Obvious That You're Not Confident** - Here's a secret you might not have thought about. *Nobody knows that you're not confident UNLESS you make it obvious.* Do you find yourself apologizing for being shy or lacking confidence? Well, it is time to stop doing that. You don't need to apologize for being shy or lacking confidence when there is a lull in the conversation or when you feel like things are getting awkward. That is *announcing* the fact that you're not a confident person. *No one has to know* unless you tell them or make it apparent. To you, it might be obvious that you're one big ball of anxiety, but to everyone else, you're a regular Joe like the rest of them. If you shout it from the rooftops, everyone is going to know about it. But if you play to cool and present a calm exterior without letting on how nervous you are, no one is ever going to know that you're silently working on overcoming your anxiety *except you*. People are not going to notice unless you tell them. If you apologize for being "shy" or "awkward," you are giving other people a label.

They can use this label to define or identify you with, and it's going to be difficult to overcome that perception if you want them to see you as a confident person later on. Apologizing for your shyness or lack of confidence is going to completely change the other person's perspective. If they didn't see you as shy before, they will now.

- **There's No Need to Set the Bar Too High** - Being confident does not mean you need to be the most outgoing person in the room. Being confident does not mean you have to dominate every single conversation you have. You can be confident and still be a good listener, letting the other person do all the talking if you wanted. Setting the bar too high will only make each social interaction seem more intense than it really is. You're psyching yourself up unnecessarily when you do that. There is no need to be a perfect conversationalist to be considered a confident person. No one is expecting you to jump from being shy to immediately extroverted when you're around people. You are the only person putting this unnecessary expectation on yourself. It's okay not to raise the bar high. When you're playing a game of tennis for the first time, you don't pick up a racket and immediately expect to play as well as the professionals do. Even more so if you have never held a ball before. There's no need to leap too far ahead of yourself. Before you can become good at tennis, you need to work on improving your swings and hits before you can start thinking about power and control. It works the same way with your conversations. If you want to learn to overcome your anxiety and become a more confident person, start by lowering the bar that you have set for yourself, and then work your way up from there. When you meet someone for the first time, keep your conversations simple and to the point. Short and sweet. It may not be the most exciting conversation in the world, but it is a start, and it is an opportunity for you to practice your conversational skills. If you know your anxiety is triggered when the bar is set too high, lower the bar and work your way up. You don't need to dazzle anyone with a stupendous story right away or charm them with irresistible charisma. Start with the basics, and you will be a confident conversationalist before you know it.

- **Watching Other People** - This strategy works best if you're in a room full of other people. Whenever you're feeling particularly anxious or nervous, pause and spend a few minutes watching the other people in the room. Focus on their body language, because it will tell you whether they're genuinely confident or not. Are they confidently making eye contact with the people they're talking to? Or are they staring into space or looking at the ground.

Are they standing comfortably? Or does their body language give you the distinct impression that they would rather be anywhere else but here. It can be oddly comforting knowing that you're not the only person out there trying to be as confident as you can be. Think you're alone when you're feeling anxious? Not at all; other people are probably in the same boat you are, except that no one is talking about it out loud. Everyone is trying to be the best version of themselves they can be. You're not alone, and whenever you feel anxious, stop and watch the other people in the room. It might surprise you to learn that nine times out of ten, they are feeling as awkward or nervous as you are. We tend to assume that we are the only ones who are feeling socially awkward and struggling with nervous anxiety. We assume that everyone around us is brimming with the confidence we wish we had. The people who genuinely love attention are only a small and select group. The rest of us tend to feel awkward, shy, and a little bit nervous when we're faced with the prospect of being in a room full of people we don't know well. By watching other people, you can take comfort in the knowledge that you are not alone. People don't seem as intimidating when you know that they share the same fears you do.

- **Own Your Nervousness** - Being nervous and anxious is nothing to be ashamed of. In fact, you should feel *proud of yourself*. Here you are, struggling with nervous anxiety, and yet you're still willing to try. You're willing to be brave and give it your best shot, and that is something not a lot of people can say that they have done. Most people might not notice how shy or nervous you are, but once in a while, someone might call you out on it. They might say something like, *"You're kind of nervous/shy."* For most socially anxious people, their first instinct is to immediately apologize for the way that they are. *You don't have to apologize.* This does not have to be something that you are ashamed of. Your shy and anxious nerves can only define you if you allow it to. What you should do instead the next time someone happens to point out you're shy or nervous is *yes, I guess I am at times*. Your nervousness does not have to define your entire personality. It is merely a small part of who you are as a person. Because that is what it is. Your nervous anxiety does not define who you are. It is only a *small part* of who you are.

CHAPTER 4
Stomping Out Your Inner Critic

No one cares about what you have to say. You're a fraud, and they will see right through you. Everyone is going to see how nervous you are in the presentation. Nobody likes you, and you know it. You're a loser; you can never get anything right. You look ugly in everything you wear. None of your clothes fit right. You've got a massive pimple on your face, and everyone is going to be staring at it. How would you feel if someone was constantly criticizing your every move? Telling you things like, "You're so stupid! You're weird! You're never going to be good enough! You're ugly!" What if there was someone standing in front of you right now criticizing you to your face? Would you stand for it? Probably not. If they push your buttons enough, you're going to fight back and stand up for yourself. From the outside, these seem like hurtful, sometimes almost cruel remarks that someone might say to you. But what if you were told that *you* were the one saying these things? Your first reaction might be to recoil in horror at the thought. You could never imagine yourself saying such things to anyone, let alone the people you cared about.

But it's true. *No one is saying these things to you. You're saying them to yourself.* You know you are a nice person, and you know you would never say these things to other people. *Yet, you would say them to yourself without a second thought.* You definitely wouldn't let anyone talk like that to any of your loved ones, family, or friends. So why would you tolerate this level of unkindness from the voice inside your head? We say such awful things to ourselves all the time, and if you're struggling with confidence, you know that you are definitely guilty of saying mean and nasty comments to yourself all the time. We've become so used to saying these nasty comments to ourselves that we don't notice them anymore. They've become almost like a bad habit. This is a habit at least 99% of the world's population are guilty of. The other 1% are the ones busy being successful.

Your Unhelpful Inner Friend

Imagine you had a friend who was by your side 24-hours a day, 7-days a week. Imagine if this friend went on and on all day long saying negative, unhelpful, hurtful things to you. Imagine this voice constantly whispering to you that you are never good enough, and you're not fooling anyone with that bravado. *You're not good enough. You're not smart enough. You're not talented enough. You're not skinny enough.* All-day long it goes on and on like this. With everything that you want to do, this voice is right there by your side, pointing out all the ways you could possibly fail and fall flat on your face. That, my friends, is your inner critic.

It also happens to be the difference between people who are confident and people who are still struggling to build confidence. The former has already learned how to control their inner critic and its self-destructive nature. If you let that little voice be stronger than your belief in yourself, you are going to have a very tough time crawling out of your insecurity hole. As for everyone else? Well, we're still struggling with our inner critic to a certain extent. Give your inner critic enough power, and it *will overpower you*. The inner critic is made up of negative thoughts, beliefs, and attitudes that oppose our best interest and diminish our self-esteem. It is our own worst enemy.

Everybody has an inner critic. That is no exception. Even the successful people have it, except that they have mastered several ways to tune this critic out, ignore it, or get rid of it entirely. Why is the inner critic your unhelpful inner friend? Because if you let that little voice be more potent than your belief in yourself, you are going to have a very tough time crawling out of your insecurity hole. We all have a nasty little inner critic that lives somewhere in our mind, and if we let it out, listen to it and start to believe everything that it tells us, we're in big trouble. If you listen to this voice, you might try to push harder and try *too hard* to prove that voice wrong that you end up burning yourself out. You end up sabotaging your relationships, perhaps even your mental and physical well being too. If you're not careful, listen to this inner voice long enough, and it is like a one way trip down the deep, dark tunnel of depression. Because you *will* end up pushing yourself too hard for one simple reason: *No matter what you do, your inner critic is going to convince you that it is never enough.* Even if you gave it 150% of your effort, your critic is going to convince you that you're still a loser. When you burn out from pushing your mind and body way too hard, your inner critic pops up and says, *"See? I told you that you're not good enough."* There's no winning with this voice. That's why they call it a critic.

Listen to this inner critical voice long enough, and you will eventually hit rock bottom. It is inevitable when all that negativity is swimming around in your head. That's not to say that your inner critic is *all bad*. Sometimes the little voice in your head can be helpful if your mindset is one that knows how to use this voice as motivation to make changes for the better. Like when your inner critic reminds you junk food is not good, or that you need to get up and start exercising if you want to look good at the family wedding next month. However, when it is not helpful, it can lead you down a dark and dangerous road. Sometimes, the little voice takes a nasty turn and does more harm than good, especially when it starts steering us towards the realm of excess negativity. When this happens, what we're engaging in is negative self-talk, and if you let it, it will bring you down so low you'll find yourself drowning in negativity with no help in sight. Depression, severe depression, chronic anxiety, a nervous system that is fried and in need of some serious care, those are all symptoms of what can happen when you listen to your inner critic for too long.

The Critic That Killed Your Confidence

If you let your inner critic run free, it will destroy your confidence even more, so if you're an emotional person. Being emotional can bring out your inner critic. We have a tendency to be hard on ourselves, and we feel like we have failed in some way. However, if you hope to master your emotions, you need to develop the confidence you need to become psychologically stronger. Being too hard on yourself will only make your emotions more difficult to regulate because you're constantly critical, and that makes your emotions fluctuate. What is even more dangerous is how being in this condition for too long will eventually lead to severe depression. The <u>World Health Organization</u> says that <u>300 million</u> people right now are suffering from depression. Yes, this condition is a global health crisis.

The trouble is that we have become so accustomed to this inner critic's nasty whisperings that we don't even notice or pay attention to it anymore. We've become so used to hearing that voice that we don't think twice about it. Sometimes the monologue can even happen on autopilot, and the musings of your inner critic can sometimes sound like a critical friend or family member who admonishes you. Negative self-talk can come in several versions. In some versions, it sounds grounded. *"I'm not the best at this task, so perhaps I should let someone else take charge, so we don't compromise the outcome. I can never do anything right! I should just give up!."* It could even sound like you're realistically appraising the situation when you say, *"I didn't get an A on my science test again, I guess I'm not good at science after all,"* although this version could quickly morph into fantasies based on fear, such as *"I'll probably never get into college if I keep scoring low grades on my tests like this!"* Yes, your inner critic can be a contributing factor to your depression (if you are struggling with depression). Imagine the damage this can do to your confidence if you let it go on. There could be a lot of reasons that contribute to why our inner critic seems to want to tear down our confidence. The first point of assessment should be your upbringing. What kind of environment were you surrounded in? Did your parents support you? Listen to you? Engage with you? Or did they tell you to stop being silly or stop making mistakes whenever you messed up? Your upbringing and the kind of environment you were surrounded in and exposed to makes a difference. The biggest culprits that kill our confidence are sometimes our own family, but we don't see it, don't want to see it, or fail to realize it. Parents and family members do occasionally criticize, perhaps when the situation calls for it but being overly critical about almost everything the child does, even when you mean well, is not good. If you grew up in this kind of environment, nothing would ever be good enough. The parent may have the best intention at heart, believing that by doing this it will help to ensure that the child does not grow up making costly mistakes in the future, but being overly critical can backfire. It may cause the child to develop insecurities and an inner critic who is always harsh, never believing that they are good enough to do anything, which can cripple them in adulthood. This is why your inner critic is the critic that killed your confidence.

With your inner critic leading the charge, you're never going to feel confident enough to want to try anything new. This negative way that you speak to yourself is damaging you from the inside. You're never going to be confident enough to rise to the challenges you face. You're never going to be confident enough to meet new people. You're never going to be confident enough in a lot of things that you do. The inner critic is going to cripple your confidence, keeping you small, and stuck in fear. Your inner critic will always run the day until you stand up to it and say *ENOUGH*. The time to stand up and stomp on your inner critic is *now*. Do it before it has a chance to do any more damage.

Say *ENOUGH* Is Enough

Don't wait until your confidence levels drop so low that it is almost non-existent anymore before you try and do something about it. The only person who can cure you of your inner critic is *yourself*. Your inner critic's negative self-talk is the underlying problem, and to become more confident, that pernicious little voice in your mind must be silenced. Your inner critic does nothing but complain, put your down, and sow needs of negativity and doubt in your mind. You don't need all of that in your life, and it is not going to benefit you in any way. You don't need that nagging little voice reminding you of how it could all go wrong and listing the many reasons you might fail. Moving forward, that inner voice must be silenced. If you don't work on the underlying issue first, you're going to find yourself back in square one each time you try to move forward.

It is time that you cast your inner critic aside so your true, confident self can shine. It begins right here by identifying what your priorities are. Make it your priority right now to become a more confident person by silencing your inner critic. Use this priority as the anchor you hold onto when challenges start billowing past you, trying to turn your world upside down. When an obstacle hits and throws all your plans in chaos, it's easy to get swept up in a negative emotional storm if you have nothing to fall back on. Being unable to identify what your priorities are will only serve to make the situation worse than it actually may be. Yes, silencing your inner critic starts with a priority. That priority is the goal you want to accomplish. It serves as a reminder of why you are working hard to silence this very unhelpful friend in your head who has become a burden.

A goal helps you stay on track when challenges are threatening to distract and misdirect you.

If you are wondering whether having a priority and a goal is necessary for this process to work, the answer is *YES*. You absolutely need this if this first step at addressing the underlying problem is going to work. Your inner critic may try to silence you and hold you back along the way, but your priorities and goals remind you of what you want to accomplish. This is the emotional support system you need to keep you staying in control. You can be surrounded by all the positivity in the world, but if you don't believe in yourself and your abilities, you're not going to go very far either. No matter what difficulties or challenges life may throw at you, remember you have the power within you to help you get through it. Part of becoming a more resilient person believes in yourself; after all, you've made it this far, haven't you? You wouldn't have if you weren't already a capable person.

The Power of Choice

Choice can be your most powerful weapon in your battle against your inner critic. In life, relationships, or work, challenges are a constant part of our life, and there will always be another challenge and another obstacle to face. But you always have a choice of how you want to react to it. It's not going to be easy, but it can be done, and that's what you need to keep reminding yourself each time you struggle to get past your inner critic. Imagine that you are now holding your hand out in front of you with your palm open and facing upward. Now, imagine that you are taking your inner critic, plucking it from your mind, and then placing it directly in the palm of your hand. Visualize this happening for a minute. Now, crush your inner critic by balling your hands tightly in a fist. Visualize yourself, *squashing it hard*. You're not ready to start crushing your inner critic.

How to Overcome Your Inner Critic for Good

Before you begin the strategies below to help you overcome your negative inner critic, there's something you need to be mindful of—your *thoughts*. Our thoughts are sometimes the things we pay attention to the least. Until they start getting out of control, that is. How easy it is for your negative thoughts to quickly start spiraling out of control before you know it. Negativity is like a disease. Once it gets a hold of you, it will do its best to keep hanging around, refusing to let go. The only way to start working on that challenge is to start practicing mindfulness and watch what you think. Recognize the kind of messages your brain is sending to itself. You might be taken aback to realize just how harmful a lot of the messages you send yourself are.

Don't let this internal enemy rob you of any more of your precious confidence and self-esteem. You are capable of great change, but the greatest change can only happen once a shift in the mindset takes place. The mind is a very powerful thing, and we can easily become a prisoner of our thoughts without even realizing that it is happening until it is too late. But that means that our minds are just as capable, just as strong enough to turn things around if we wanted it to. It's time to turn the tables on your inner critic, and this is what you need to do:

- **Turn Your Critic Into A Character** - Visualize your inner critic again as a separate entity. Imagine that they were not living inside your head. Imagine they were a real person. Who is your inner critic? What do they look like? Are they male or female? Tall? Short? Imagine your inner critic in such detail that they almost become like another person altogether. Turning your inner critic into a character is an important step in shutting it down for good because when you imagine your inner critic as someone else, you can slowly begin distancing yourself from them. In the same way, you would stay away from a toxic person. Your confident self and your inner critic cannot co-exist. They must become two separate entities if you want to become a more confident person.
- **Fight Back Against Your Inner Critic** - Don't let your inner critic walk all over you. Don't let it convince you that you're not good enough or worthy. Whenever your inner critic tries to say something that tears down your confidence, fight back against it with one very simple question: *Why?* Each time you have a bad thought, stop and ask your critic why? What evidence do you have that will lead you to believe what your critic is trying to convince you of. You'll need to put on your analytical thinking cap here and fight your inner critic with good old fashion logic. Criticizing yourself is something you've done long enough. This time, it's time to fight your critic in the form of questions. It might surprise you to find the more you try to justify your negative thoughts with evidence or facts, the more you'll struggle. Why? Because what your inner critic is trying to convince you of is *not* based on facts. It's not real. As your inner critic stumbles and fumbles, trying to find an answer to your rebuttals, it's time to move onto the next point.
- **Slamming the Door Shut** - Remember how you're supposed to picture your inner critic as a separate person? Well, this is where you get to have a little bit of fun. If you have always wondered what it feels like to slam the door shut on someone you disliked, now is your chance to do it. Well, not really, but close enough. Slamming the door shut on your inner critic is going to feel so good. It helps if you imagine your inner critic as an

annoying salesperson who comes knocking on your door at the most inconvenient times. You would tell them, *"Nope, sorry, not interested,"* and close the door. Do the same thing to your inner critic. Slam the door shut on this annoying entity that is trying to steal your confidence. Your inner critic is knocking on your mental door, coming to plant these seeds of doubt, hoping to steal your confidence away. What are you doing? Getting ready to slam the door shut. That is what you are doing.

- **Replace Your Negative Thoughts Like You Replace Old Clothes** - Toss them out. Toss them out by replacing your negative thoughts with a positive one instead. For every negative thought you have, think *two* happy thoughts to counteract it. This is the only effective technique needed to squash that inner critic inside you. If you don't do anything about it, the negative thoughts in your head are only going to steadily ruin your success a little bit at a time if you don't do something to stop it. It's important to start acknowledging what you say to yourself. You're doing it all the time anyway, except we're not mindful of these thoughts. Listen to the way you talk to yourself. Identify what your unhelpful thoughts are and separate them from the negative ones. Yes, there is a difference between the two. Not all negative thoughts are necessarily bad. An example of a negative thought is, *"I'm stressed and frustrated, but I know it will get easier,"* while an unhelp thought would be, *"I hate my current job, and I never want to go back to that office again!"* Once you begin noticing the messages you send, it's time to replace the less than desirable ones. What you could do, for example, is choose to either see a setback as a failure or acknowledge that they can sometimes be opportunities in disguise. Instead of seeing failure as an indication that you're not good enough, see failure as a teacher you learn from. It all depends on how you look at it. Train your mind to look at this from a positive point of view. See the bright side and the good of every situation, and you will find that often things may not be as bleak as it initially seems. You need to start paying attention to your thoughts because this is where you start making the necessary changes needed to change the way you think. When we're not mindful of the changes in our thoughts, the negativity makes us feel worse, and it becomes even more difficult to focus. By paying attention to the thoughts that creep into your head, you're instantly more attuned to what those thoughts are and how they make you feel. If it is bad for you or going to affect your confidence levels, you need to remove these thoughts from your life for good.
- **Focusing on Nothing But the Facts** - Once again, facts are going to be your greatest weapon in this step. If a thought is not

valid and based on facts, push back against these thoughts by focusing on the information that you know. Always go back to the facts that you know and cross-reference that with your thoughts. Ask yourself, "Am I basing this on fact? Or speculation?". Replace these unhelpful thoughts with concrete facts to support your argument and make it believable. The facts never lie, and focusing on this is one way of reigning in your thoughts to keep them from spiraling out of control. Reframe your mindset to look at the areas of your life or your personality that you are not satisfied with just yet and think about what you can do to change that. Instead of beating yourself up and letting your inner critic put you down, challenge yourself to think about how you can change those areas, and start believing in yourself. Believe in your abilities. Believe that this stressful period is not going to last forever. The storm will pass, and you need to believe you are strong enough to stick it out.

- **Love Yourself** - Love yourself enough to the point that you feel guilty for even thinking about these bad thoughts about yourself. Be happy and satisfied with who you are—choosing to be happy means being okay with where you are in life, even if it is not necessarily where you want to be just yet. The answer to that is much easier when you've identified a sense of purpose, something you can use as an anchor that keeps you rooted and wavering so your stress will never get the best of you. You can certainly get through anything with the right attitude and positive beliefs backing you up. If you could do it then, there is nothing stopping you from doing the same thing again except a whole bunch of excuses your inner critic has just fed you with. You need to love yourself, or rather, learn to love yourself again because you are worth it, and your inner critic has made you forget who you are and how much you are worth. Are you going to let your negative emotions and thoughts define who you are and dictate what your life should be? Or do you want more out of this one life that you have to live? Loving yourself is the only way you're ever going to have the courage to be brave enough to stand up for yourself. If you don't love yourself, you're sending a clear message to your inner critic that you're easily dominated. You need to love yourself first and foremost and use the strength of that love to help you develop your confidence. A person who loves themselves will never allow themselves to be treated with anything less than respect. The decision is yours to be as positive or as negative as you want to be in the face of stress.
- **Be Comfortable Talking About Your Feelings** - Don't forget that the brain has a limited storage space capacity. All those thoughts need to go somewhere, or they're going to get bigger and

bigger, making it feel like your head is about to explode at the next trigger. Even if those emotions are uncomfortable or something you would prefer not to deal with, do it anyway because it is still a part of who you are. It can be hard to remain positive all the time, especially when you've experienced a setback or things are not going according to plan. When you let your emotions out, you're going to feel so much better. Like a huge weight has been lifted off your chest. Talking about things can be a very liberating feeling. It is time you started living the life that you were meant to live. Don't be afraid to talk about your emotions when you need to. Don't be afraid to talk about your emotions. Don't keep your emotions bottled up inside. Learn to be okay with expressing yourself and letting it all out. Your emotions are not your enemy, so start embracing them instead of resisting them. One of the unspoken things we yearn for is a deep connection to others. But in order to develop that deep connection, we must be able to openly share ourselves with others. We need to build enough trust to let others in, or we will always feel alone.

- **I Don't Have to Be Perfect** - Let this be the answer you always give your inner critic from now on when it tries to convince you that you're not worth it. Push back against your inner critic with this sentence whenever it tries to tell you that you're going to fail if you try. *You don't have to be perfect.* No one in this world is perfect, not even the successful people out there today. They've all failed and fallen several times along the way, made mistakes they wished they hadn't, but they still didn't let their inner critic stop them or rob them of their confidence. Why? Because they knew that they did not have to be perfect. You don't have to be perfect before you're worthy of love. You don't have to be perfect before you can strike up a conversation with someone. You don't have to be perfect before you start going after that promotion at work that you want. *You don't have to be perfect because no one is.* Let that sink in and let that be one of the anchors you hold onto whenever your inner critic tries to lead you astray. You are doing your best, and that is all anyone can do.

Preaching Positivity

In fact, why not take a leaf out of the motivational speaker's book and do what they do? At every opportunity, jump at the chance to talk about positivity. Imagine you're like a motivational speaker, and it's now your mission to spread positivity at every chance you get. Especially when you're interacting with someone who needs it and who may be struggling to overcome negativity too, you may not be a motivational speaker in a professional capacity, but that doesn't mean you can't take a leaf out of their book and preach and teach too. If your mind is capable of complaining and being negative without even thinking about it, you can certainly change your brain and your thoughts, so it goes in the opposite direction too.

If you think you can't be a positive person because of the mistakes you have made, *think again*. The control is always in your hands, and the way you feel says a lot about what you choose to focus on. Focus on your strengths and all the other trials you've managed to overcome before. You got through those, and you are much stronger because of it. Remember, all you can do is your best, and you need to let that be enough. Look at it this way, if you tried and you failed, that means you were *brave enough* to try and do something. That is something you should absolutely be proud of. You may not have succeeded today, but the point is that you tried, and that is something your inner critic can never take away from you.

CHAPTER 5
Building A Tougher Character

Are you resilient? After you get knocked down, do you pick yourself back up? Getting back up on your feet again after a particularly tough challenge is not always the easiest thing in the world. In fact, it is going to feel like a nearly impossible task if you don't have a tough character alongside confidence. Mentally tough and resilient people don't happen overnight, and they don't magically appear one day. Nor were they born with it. It is a quality which they worked hard at building every day to get to where they are right now. It took hard work, self-discipline, willpower, and the determination to never back down and never say die. When things got tough, they took that as an opportunity to prove to themselves just what they were made of, and over time, the resilience and toughness became a part of who they were. But if you ask them whether it was all worth it, their answer will always be a resounding *yes*.

When you've got a tough character and confidence on your side, you're much happier. You're happier because you are not afraid to go after what your heart desires. You're happier because you're willing to take risks, and you know that nothing feels better than seeing those risks pay off in a big way. You're happier because you're not afraid to go out there and live the life that you want on your own terms. You're happier because you are not afraid of failure anymore when you know how to stand up again every time you've been knocked down. You're happier because you have the confidence and the resilience to do all of the above and so much more. Resilience and confidence are life-changing traits you can and should be focused on developing.

Resilience and Why We Need It

If you dare to dream big and you want to go after your goals, you are going to fall down. Not once, not twice, but several times along the way before you can cross that finish line. You're going to cry, you're going to feel stressed and frustrated, and you're going to be pushed to your limits. That is because nothing that is worth having is ever going to come easily. You have to *earn* the life that you want, and it is going to push you to your breaking point. But if you can see it through and survive, everything is going to be worth the effort and the struggle. The problem is, it is hard to survive the emotional, mental, and sometimes physical turmoil that these challenges will present you with if you are not mentally tough, resilient, and confident.

The struggles are how you know that you are on the right track, that you are living your life to the fullest and going for the big goals. It is completely okay to fail. It is *good* if you fail once or twice along the way. The challenges are how you know that you are giving meaning to your life, that your life has a purpose and a goal. Where most of us struggle is how to pick ourselves back up again faster and with double the persistence. Staying stuck in the self-criticism and the self-doubt that these trials and tribulations will sometimes present you with are the reasons why you need a tougher character and confidence on your side. You do need failure, and you do need hardships because that is how we learn and grow. What you are trying to do now is figure out a way to bounce back quickly so you can keep the momentum going.

The easiest way to define resilience is the ability to bounce back to your original state after being put through the wringer. When challenges push you, pull you, stretch you, and turn your emotions upside down, that ability to quickly recover your focus and determination, that ability to keep going is how you define resilience. That is how you know you have a tougher character that won't quit at the first sign of hardship. A tough character gives you the ability to keep growing and keep putting one foot in front of the other when you feel like quitting the most. It is the discipline to stay focused despite what you may be going through and the determination to never give up.

What Resilient People Do

When they get their butts kicked, resilient and tough people, they embrace their emotions. When they get rejected and face disappointments, they embrace their feelings. They acknowledge all the emotions that may be running through them, and they embrace those emotions rather than deny them. It's natural to want to resist negative emotions. They're unpleasant, but you now need to embrace them just as you would with the emotions that make you feel good. Acknowledge that they're there, and don't fight it off. Resisting them will only diminish your confidence in your ability to remain in control, and a lack of confidence is going to work against you as an attempt to make progress. Resilient people don't jump immediately into thinking positively or using affirmations to help them let go of the hurt and pain they're experiencing. They take the time they need to embrace those emotions and process them properly.

When you try to move on too quickly, you're not addressing your emotions properly. You're numbing, repressing, or bottling up your emotions, and that is never a healthy thing to do. You need to create a safe space for yourself to feel these emotions, even if they are hard, and even if you don't want to think about them. Openly acknowledge that you feel the way you do; there's nothing to be ashamed of. Analyze and think about the significance of that emotion in relation to the situation that you find yourself in. Why do you feel this way? What has triggered such a response? When someone has made you angry, for example, instead of resisting the emotion, acknowledge your anger at the circumstances that

triggered it. You are allowed to feel disappointed, hurt, and frustrated. You are allowed to feel pain. Your emotions are not something to be ashamed of, even though some emotions are unpleasant to deal with.
Tough personalities embrace all of these emotions, good and bad, and they let them all in. The difference between them and other, less confident people, are that these tougher personalities don't wallow in their misery. They embrace it when the situation sucks. They embrace it when they feel hurt and disappointed. They embrace and then move on. How do they seem to move on without being stuck for too long? They know those feelings they have are temporary. They know the disappointment is temporary. They know that feeling hurt and pain is temporary. The only way those feelings are going to become permanent is if you allow them to stay. There is a quote that goes like this: *"Your emotions are like the waves of the ocean. You can't stop them from coming, but you can choose which wave you want to surf"*. This quote is a profound reminder that you will never be able to prevent your emotions, but you can choose how you're going to let it affect you. There is another old saying that goes: *"It's not what happens to you, but rather how you choose to respond to it that matters."* This is very true indeed. It is the way you have chosen to respond that has led you to this point in your life, where you are right now.
This is how confident people manage to stay resilient and tough, no matter what happens to them. They know that it comes down to learning how to regulate and master your emotions. It is what they do every single day and how they keep themselves ahead of everyone else. This is how they ensure that no matter what happens, they never let challenges rob them of their confidence. They observe their feelings and reflect on them. It is easy to fall out of touch with ourselves in this hectic world that we live in. With the hectic lives we juggle, trying to manage one thing after another, taking care of ourselves often falls by the wayside, and we lose that connection to our innermost feelings. The way you chose to respond was influenced by your perception and interpretation of the circumstances that happened in your life. When you're unable to manage your emotions properly, that's when you make impulsive decisions that often result in regret later on.
Mentally tough and resilient individuals never get stuck in their emotions for too long because they know the discomfort is not going to last. They know that they will move through whatever it is they are feeling, and they will be stronger because of it. This knowledge helps them stay calm enough to keep themselves focused on the bigger picture and keeps their confidence intact. What most people choose to do is the easier, more convenient thing. Instead of learning how to focus on their emotions, they choose to brush it aside, ignore, or deny their emotions completely. They may even distract themselves from those feelings by doing something else. The more you deny your feelings, though, the harder it

becomes to manage them later on. Bottling up your emotions and hoping they will just go away on its own has never proven to be an effective strategy. If it were, there would be no such thing as emotional outbursts. Another thing that resilient people do is show understanding, compassion, and kindness to themselves. They don't have themselves for having these emotions. They're *kind* to themselves *because* they have these emotions. They don't take pity on themselves or think of themselves as the victim, which is what most other people tend to do. Feeling sorry for yourself when your emotions have gotten out of hand is not beneficial. Yes, you feel sorry and regret what's been done. You wish you would have handled the situation better, but feeling sorry for yourself is not going to change what has happened. Negativity will one serve to make your emotions spiral even more out of control than they already are. Things always seem ten times when you're down in the dumps, so it's time to get rid of this habit and start taking accountability for your emotions.

Resilient and confident people are never looking to shift the blame. They never try to point the finger or blame someone else for the way they feel. If you're always looking for an opportunity to blame someone else, to eagerly shift the blame, so you don't have to feel as bad about losing control, you need to keep working on your emotional intelligence as well as your confidence. The way you choose to react is always a decision that lies with you. No one forced you into it; that was completely your decision and yours alone. Resilient and confident people show understanding toward themselves. They understand that they are allowed to feel disappointed and frustrated sometimes, and it is okay to feel everything that they feel. They love themselves enough to treat themselves with kindness and to treat themselves with kindness, even in the face of disappointments. It is not a bad thing to love yourself, and no one should make you feel guilty about it. If you are going to constantly rely on others to feel worthy, you will never become the improved version of yourself that you long to be. Self- love is not to be confused with narcissism. Narcissism is being in love with yourself, which is a different matter altogether. Self-love is a reminder to yourself that you're good enough the way you are, and you deserve to have good things happen to you too. If you have no problem telling people you love how amazing and incredible they are, and how deserving they are of love, why not do the same for yourself? For happiness to exist long-term, self-love needs to be present.

Confidence Requires Mental Toughness

When the going gets tough, it can be tempting to give in to the desire to quit, admit defeat, and run away. But those are the instincts you need to battle against, and it is a battle you must not lose. The minute you do, your hope of being tougher mentally diminishes just a little bit more with each defeat. Do not give in to fear, because you are capable of so much more than you give yourself credit for; you have overcome difficult situations in the past, you need to now make it a habit of doing it all the time.

Resilience Is A Character Trait

There are several phrases that could be used to describe someone. Hard-working, generous, compassionate, friendly, honest, wise, confident, and the list goes on. If you were to describe yourself in one word, what would it be? Is it a description that you would be happy to be associated with? Picture your ideal self. Visualize it as though it has already happened, and you are the person that you want to be. What values do you see yourself having? If you were looking at yourself from a third-person point of view, would you be happy with the character traits that you see? Be crystal clear about the vision, and it will help you believe that you are everything that you want to be. Building a tougher character means never giving in to the urge to run away when things get hard.

Resilience Is Built Through A Willingness to Change

Bruce Lee, one of the most famous martial artists in history, was known for encouraging his students and followers to emulate water. While most people saw water as a sign of weakness, Lee, on the other hand, saw water as the ultimate sign of strength. He was always encouraging everyone to be just like water because water can never be snapped. In his own words, Lee said that everyone should be like water because it is soft, resilient, and formless. Water was one of the strongest existing elements here on Earth because of its very nature and ability to move, adapt, and elude when needed. Instead of fighting and resisting, water adapts.
Lee was always someone who was determined to look forward and keep moving, just like water did. Lee was someone who lived fiercely and intensely in his present moment. He was always working on improving himself by gathering experiences and knowledge that would help him grow into a better and wiser person. One of his philosophies was that a person needs to keep on flowing just like the water did because water that runs can never grow stale. Bruce Lee was a firm believer that everyone could learn to overcome the obstacles in the way that water did. Instead of fighting and resisting the challenges that come our way, Bruce Lee believed that we should embrace those challenges and learn to move alongside the obstacles that come into our path. It is only in this way that everyone could silently conquer their obstacles. Throughout his life, Lee based a lot of his philosophy on emulating the movement and the flow of the river. He never clung to the circumstances of his past; instead, he chose to let his current existence take him to unknown places because he

was willing to adapt when he needed to. He never clung onto the past, or let it hold him back,

Resilience Is Built Through Gratitude

Being grateful helps remind you that you should stop and remember to live in the present. Not just live in the moment, but be grateful for it and everything good that has happened to you as of that moment. This is a complete opposite of what a lack of confidence will encourage. Poor confidence does nothing but plague you with stress and worries, whereas gratitude teaches and reminds you that you have a lot to be grateful for if you really think about it. When you have so much to be thankful and grateful for, worries and challenges seem to bother you a lot less. Not only does gratitude actively remind you of the things you have to be grateful for, but when you actively remind yourself of all the good experiences you have in your life, it eventually helps to magnify positive thoughts, and soon, the positive thoughts will eventually be strong enough to overpower any negative and toxic emotions that might be holding you back from becoming the confident person you should be. Be grateful every single day. It makes you tougher and less prone to stress.

Steps to A More Resilient and Confident You

Life is going to toss you all sorts of curveballs, and the only way you're going to make it through that with your confidence intact is if you work on becoming resilient and tough. Build that strong character that is going to make you as tough as nails. Tough enough to handle even the most difficult challenges you have ever faced up to this point. These steps are going to make a difference in your life, and this is what you need to do:

- **Develop A Positive Way of Talking to Yourself** - When things aren't going your way, and you are being pushed to your limits to the point of wanting to give up, *how do you talk to yourself through this tough time?* Do you motivate and encourage yourself? Treat yourself with kindness? Or do you kick yourself and tell yourself what a massive disappointment you are? What sort of language do you use when you're talking yourself through these tough times? The way you talk to yourself should be encouraging, motivating, and kind. It should use language that makes sense, a language that is compassionate. You're already feeling pretty terrible that something didn't work out the way that you hoped; you don't have to kick yourself when you're already down. You wouldn't kick someone else when they were already feeling at their lowest point, so why do it to yourself? Be *kind* because it goes a long way toward your self-esteem and confidence. Be kind because you don't deserve to be treated unkindly when you know you have already tried your best. When you've fallen, think about what you would love to hear from a friend or loved one. What could they say to you that would make you feel loved and supported during this tough time? *That* is the kind of language you should be using on yourself. You need to know how to pick yourself up again in the *right manner* whenever you have fallen because you are going to fall many times. It is going to get to you if you don't have a healthy coping mechanism. It's time to put the inner critic on mute and let your self-talk become emotionally empowering and inspiring instead. If you don't learn how to tune out the negative voice you might have become so accustomed to, your problems and challenges are always going to seem magnified and worse than they are. Everything is going to feel like a big deal when you don't have a healthy coping mechanism. Let the way you talk to yourself be filled with love and support.

- **Detach from Your Thoughts -** Your thoughts will take you on an emotional roller coaster if you leave them in charge. Your thoughts will try to convince you of things that aren't true. When your thoughts begin to feel like they're overpowering you, your sense of control begins to slip away, and that only causes you to feel even more frustrated and miserable at the way things are going. Your thoughts are always going to try and play tricks on you because that is what your inner critic loves to do. Play games with your mind and convince you that all your worst fears are true, and there is nothing you can do to change that. Your mind is your most powerful weapon of change to achieve success in everything that you do in life. If you want your life to change, to think better, do better, and achieve more, then you need to begin taking ownership of your thoughts and change the way you think. Nothing is going to change unless you make the choice to do it. To be accountable and take ownership of your mind and your thoughts. To be a problem solver instead of a downer and changing your mindset is what you need for change is going to get you there. Reframing your point of view is essentially changing your mindset. A mind over matter exercise. If you put your mind to it, you can do it. *Your feelings are not facts. They are your emotions*. Emotions are volatile, and they will shift and change at the drop of a hat. Why allow yourself to believe these thoughts are true? It is only going to distress you if you do. You need to learn to detach from your thoughts. Your negative thoughts do not define who you are and what you can do. Don't give them this kind of power over you and your confidence. You don't need to take your thoughts seriously. You don't need to pay attention or engage with every thought that pops into your head, especially if the negative ones. You don't need to perceive every thought you

have is the truth. You are not your thoughts. You don't have to ignore or deny your thoughts, but don't let yourself get swept up by them until you start losing confidence.
- **Minding Your Language** - Let's dig a little deeper about the language we use when we're going through particularly tough times. The language that we use most often determines our brain's fundamental capacities and the automatic physiological we are subjected to because of that language. Words can be a powerful force of good when used for the right reasons, but on the other end of the spectrum, it can be used to inflict great harm and pain. The old adage about how the pen is mightier than the sword stems from the very real fact that words can cause a great deal of pain and leave scars so deep they might never fully recover. English philosopher and writer Aldous Huxley once said words are like an X-ray. When words are used in negative ways, these words can pierce through almost everything. Dignity, self-esteem, even the identity of another can be threatened with the right kind of words. Being aware of the way we use our words is one of the most crucial factors that will determine the state of our emotional wellness. In other words, if you want to be happy, you need to be using the right words and language. We rely on language to interpret the different sensations, events, and experiences we undergo. We use language to put a name to the emotion that we're feeling at the time. The different words that we use create different physiological responses. For example, two people could be going through the same situation. When one person says, *"It could have been worse,"* while the other person says, *"This is the worst thing that could have ever happened to me."* The first individual is going to be the one with a better, slightly happier emotional well being by simply phrasing the same situation using different words. Rephrase the language you use so that you are embracing your emotions for what they are instead of trying to deny their presence. Use your words to understand your negative emotions instead of treating them like an enemy. Everything is temporary and impermanent, even your emotions, so mind your language to keep your confidence intact.
- **Accepting the Fact That Life *Is Hard*** - It may not be what you want to hear, but it is a fact you can't deny. Life is hard. Denying it is not going to make it any easier. Getting worked up over the hardship is not going to change anything. Life is hard, and it has its moments. Some people are going through harder times than others. Life is not perfect. Nobody is perfect, no matter how hard they try to make it seem like they are. Life is hard, and no one has an easy time of it. Everyone goes through hard times, and you're not alone in this. That's why self-love and self-

acceptance can be a challenge. Hard times will definitely try to beat you down, and it takes a lot of courage and inner strength to push back against it. But if you believe in yourself, you're already winning. Life will have its ups and downs. It is not always going to be hard, and it is not always going to be easy. That is the way it is, and the sooner we embrace it, the easier it will be when you're not pushing back, fighting, and resisting against life. Instead of being angry about it or hating it, embracing it will make you more willing to go through life. This willingness and open-mindedness is the key to staying focused and confident throughout the hard parts.

- **Be Responsible for Your Choices** - To overcome the victim mentality, you need to take a step back. One of the biggest challenges we all face is taking responsibility and being accountable for our own emotions and our choices. It is always easier to point the finger at someone else, to blame others, and claim they are responsible for what has happened. These options are easier than having to look inside ourselves and face the unpleasant fact that we may have a bigger role to play in our misery. Believing and blaming others for your misery is the easier pill to swallow rather than having to admit that you are the cause of your unhappiness. Bad things happen; that's a part of life and the way it works. Sometimes we see it coming, other times we don't. Bad things can happen to anyone, anytime, anywhere. However, believing that these thoughts are done to you will trap you in a victim mentality. It distracts you from the truth, which is that these patterns of thought are simply a matter of habit. The trouble is most people tend to be too harsh on themselves. You're not trapped in a prison; you're merely trapped in a bad habit. You see, the mind is like the needle of a compass. It can only point in a single direction at a time. This means that we're only meant to think and focus on one thought at a time. This fact is going to be the secret to successfully shifting your thoughts away from negativity because you cannot think of a negative and positive thought at the same time. The victim mentality will lead you to believe that the world is out to get you; everything always happens to you. The problem always lies outward, and you don't think about looking inward for a source and solution. A "victim" will go through their entire lives blaming someone else or something else for where they are in life. No surprise why this paradigm sits on the negative end. As long as you keep blaming something or someone else for what's going on in your life, you will never have the power to change it. As long as you keep blaming, your mind will never have enough power or resources to overcome negativity. *You always have a choice. Always.*

- **Be Willing to Be Uncomfortable** - It is the only way you are going to grow and learn. You cannot become a better version of yourself if you are not willing to go through a little bit of discomfort. Life can't be smooth sailing all the way, although we certainly wished that it could. If you're not willing to put yourself through the discomfort in order to get better, then you're never going to get better. That is the simple truth. You can't let fear make your decisions for you. You're not living to your full potential when you allow fear to cripple your motivation. You're not living when fear stops you from learning and developing the new skills you need to grow as a person. You're not living when you make poor decisions based on your fearful emotions. *You need to make the best decisions for yourself.* Nobody likes going through hard times and challenges, but it is these challenges that make us who we are. Just remember that the difficulties you encounter in your life are not a threat. They may be uncomfortable, but they are not a threat. They may not be pleasant, but they are not a threat. If they are not a threat, they don't have the power to affect your confidence *unless* you allow them to.

CHAPTER 6
It's Okay To Look After Yourself

If you have ever compared yourself to someone else and felt bad about yourself, nod your head in agreement. If you decided that they were better than you and your confidence took a nosedive because of that comparison, nod your head in agreement. If you ever felt like you were never good enough when you look around at everyone else around you, nod your head. If you're not taking care of yourself and your happiness the way that you should be, nod your head.

When you're young, other people are in charge of looking after you. Parents, guardians, other family members, babysitters, teachers, aunts, uncles, and grandparents who would remind you to look after yourself. Get enough rest, make sure you're eating all your fruits and vegetables, staying safe; they would be there to remind you of these things because they were responsible for your wellbeing. They affirm us, so we believe we're good enough, and we have what it takes to succeed. They support us so that we have the happiest childhood growing up by making sure we are safe and healthy. They set boundaries for us to make sure we are protected. But who looks after our wellbeing once we hit adulthood? *You are.* You are now responsible for your own affirming words and thoughts. You are not responsible for making sure you are well looked after, that your boundaries are in place, so you're safe, protected, and happy. You are now responsible for your own needs. You are now responsible for being your own cheerleader, and if you neglect all of the above, your confidence is going to be one of the elements that suffer the consequences.

The constant comparison to others, trying to figure out where you fit in within your social circle, thinking about where your life is going and whether you're living your life to the fullest, all of those things can have a big impact on the way that we feel. The outside world is filled with a lot of stress, and if you don't do anything to look after yourself, that stress is going to take its toll on you.

What Does Self-Care Mean

This is not a new concept. In fact, it has been the buzzword for a while now, and you've probably heard this term several times. People talk about it all the time on social media, blogs, podcasts, motivational speeches, inspirational books, even among people you might know in general. The best way to define self-care would be a *"happy, healthy, functional, and productive relationship with yourself."* When you're in a relationship with a partner, you're always so eager and willing to do things for the relationship to keep it healthy and happy. Well, self-care is pretty much the same thing except this time, you're going to be doing all those things for *yourself*. This is a term we have been hearing a lot in recent years. Mostly because people are finally beginning to realize how important it is to do things for yourself.

Now, it is important to highlight here that self-care and *self-love* are not the same things. Self-care is about taking action to improve or preserve your health. It is about the things you do to make yourself feel better. Some examples of this could include self-pampering, taking a nap when you're tired, taking a bath, going for a massage. Self-love, on the other hand, is focused on your regard for your own happiness and wellbeing. It is the way you see yourself. Both of these are essential to your happiness, and you need both of them to become a more confident person. You need to do things to look after yourself, and at the same time, you also need to pay attention to how you see yourself, not how others perceive you. Your opinion of yourself needs to be entirely yours, not what other people say about you. Self-love and self-care are different for everyone, and it's easy to see why these two concepts could be mistaken for the same thing. *"I must love myself if I'm going to treat myself to a nice weekend relaxing at the spa."* Right? Not necessarily, though. You could be doing all those things to look after yourself but still be saddled with low self-esteem because you don't think you're worthy. Taking care of yourself does not mean you accept your flaws or where you are in life and how happy you are with your accomplishments. You could be treating yourself to all the self-care techniques in the world but still be filled with an emptiness inside. If you're struggling to think about at least 5 things that you love about yourself, you need to work on strengthening that self-love aspect too. You can't be confident if you don't genuinely love who you are.

Are You Looking After Yourself?

What do you do right now to take care of yourself? Do you practice self-care? Ask most people this question, and you might be met with vague answers like, *"I like to read if I have the time. I get a pedicure once in a while. I go to the gym and try to eat healthily. I like to binge-watch something on Netflix during the weekends and stay in my pajamas."* Some people might even give you a blank stare in response to that question about what you do to take care of yourself. Beyond the little things here and there that we do for ourselves occasionally, most of us are not that great at taking care of ourselves. We certainly don't do it enough on a daily basis, and when we do, *we feel guilty about it*. We feel bad for taking time off to look after ourselves, and this is a sign of poor confidence. When you believe that you are *not worth* spending the time and energy on, you're not a confident person. You're not someone who practices self-love because you feel bad about looking after yourself.

A sure sign that you're not practicing self-care the way that you should is when you're willing to do this for other people, even if it means neglecting your own needs. You'll do it for them, but if you had to do the same for yourself, you would feel bad about it. You would be reluctant to do it because it feels selfish. If someone you cared about asked you to do something for them, you would do it anyway, even if you didn't feel like it. When you're in a relationship with someone you love, you encourage them to be the best version of themselves every day. We do an excellent job of making sure that the people in our lives know without a doubt that they matter to us. But when it comes to ourselves, why does the love stop? Why do we choose to neglect the most important relationship of all? The relationship that we have with *ourselves*. Why are we so willing to affirm, nurture, and protect the people we love, but we don't do it for ourselves? When we were young kids, it never crossed our minds that we weren't worthy enough. We never thought that we were not worth it. We never questioned our own value and worth. But we do it as adults. Why? Because for some strange reason or another, we've been led to believe that self-care is *selfish*.

Is It Selfish?

Self-care is *not selfish*. You can't pour from an empty cup. Self-care is never a selfish thing, and it's time to drop this frame of mind. It is never going to do you any good to constantly compare yourself to others. Their story is not the same as yours. You have your unique offerings based on your strengths, and that's where you draw on your confidence to see it through. When you need a break or a time-out, take it. Don't hesitate, don't feel bad, don't dwell on the guilt you feel. There's no reason to feel guilty about taking the time you need to look after your mental, physical, and emotional wellbeing. When you need a time-out or some self-care, take it. Don't let anyone make you feel bad for taking the time to care for the most important person you know. *Yourself.*
Right now, *you* are the most neglected person that you know. When was the last time you did something for yourself without feeling guilty about it? Self-care is part of learning who you are and knowing when you need to step back and take a breath. What do you need to feel recharged and connected with yourself again? Spending a few hours in your favorite spot curled up with a book? A nice, warm bath at the end of a long day? Learning about yourself is going to be a tough journey, and it is important to practice self-care along the way. It keeps your thoughts from becoming scattered and erratic whenever you're feeling the stress. No one should have to be made to feel guilty about practicing self-care. Self-care is self-help. On every flight, as the plane is getting ready for take-off, the air stewards and stewardesses go through the steps of their safety demonstration. In it, they advise in the event of an emergency that you put your oxygen mask on first before assisting others under your care.

The same thing works with self-help. Before you can help others, you need to help yourself first.

Self-care is often confused for selfishness or self-indulgence. This explains why we feel bad about doing something for ourselves. We think we're being selfish by putting our needs first, but nothing could be further from the truth. Self-care is neither of those things; it is a process of intentionally giving yourself the help that your mind, body, and soul needs. *It's okay* to give yourself the weekend to rest and recover from a busy and hectic week. This shouldn't be a process you only do once in a blue moon. Rest and relaxation is something that needs to be regularly. Every week, in fact. You spend a lot of the week working hard, sometimes pushing yourself beyond your limits. Your body and mind need time to recharge and recover after that, and this needs to become a self-help habit you make part of your regular ritual. *It's okay* to do what makes you feel good, because why not? Thinking we "don't deserve it" is the wrong mentality to adopt. It is not going to do you any favors if you keep feeling guilty each time you do something for yourself. It's time to start believing that you are worthy. Feeling good about yourself yields important mental and physical health benefits. When we feel great, we're less stressed, and our mental and physical health doesn't suffer the consequences as much.

Kindness and self-compassion are two important self-care qualities that you need to adopt. No one else can do this part for you. Be kind to yourself and watch what a difference it can make when you stop blaming yourself or beating yourself up, thinking that you are not worth the trouble.

The Magic of Putting Yourself First

Self-care is not selfish. Let that thought become ingrained in your mind. When you put yourself first, you will have so much more to give to yourself, your goal, your career, and the people around you. Every facet of your life will seem to blossom and grow when you take the time to prioritize yourself. When you practice self-care, this is what happens:

- **You Become Someone Who Gives More** - It's harder for you to offer your help to other people when you're not in a good place yourself. Life can be stressful. That's the world that we live in today. It's face-paced, it's on the move, it changes every minute, and we have to balance more on our plate these days than we had to several years ago. Personal life, family, work, relationships, friendships, financial responsibilities, other responsibilities. It's a lot to handle, and if we don't proactively take steps to take care of ourselves, the pressure can easily get to us. If you're feeling stressed and overwhelmed, there is no way you're going to be focused or strong enough to help anyone else. It is going to feel like a *huge* effort to help anyone else when it feels like you need help too. If you're someone who loves to lend a helping hand, this

is going to make you feel guilty, and that guilt is only going to make you even more stressed than you already are. Guilt is not the best emotion to carry around with you when you're trying to work on building your confidence.
- **Your Happiness Is Going to Be Contagious** - When you're happy, it is going to show. The people who spend the most time with you are going to see and feel your happiness. Even a smile is going to go a long way when you're feeling buoyant and confident. A happy and positive attitude is always going to transcend and overflow into the other areas of your life. Other people love being around people who are happy and confident, and when you embody both these qualities because you're taking care of yourself and your needs, you're going to attract more good people into your life. They're going to be drawn to you and your infectious happiness. Self-care reminds you that there are good things to look forward to in your life, something to feel happy and positive about. If you are going to maintain the motivation you need to keep going, it is very important that you find ways to stay positive, no matter what obstacles you may face. When you take time to take care of yourself and destress, everything else in your life will fall into place.
- **You're Going to Become A Lot More Grateful and Motivated** - Positive energy in your life goes a long way. It keeps you motivated, passionate about your life, enthusiastic, and grateful. Self-care teaches you to count your blessings more and to be grateful for all the little things you get to do. So often, we take for granted how good we have it in life. Eating three full meals a day. Going to a spa when we feel the need to unwind. Coming back to a comfortable home and relaxing in front of the TV at the end of a long day. There are people out there who don't even know where their next meal is coming from. They don't have the luxury of being able to spend money on certain self-care measures, even if they wanted to. Practicing self-care is an exercise that makes you actively think about the good things happening in your life. That despite the difficult day you might have had, there were still moments of positivity in it that brought a smile to your face. Taking the time to count your blessings is one approach to achieving more balance in your life. It's hard to be negative and grateful at the same time. When you're a lot more relaxed and happy, you become a lot more motivated to reach your goals. When other people see how motivated you've become to reach your goals, you just might be the inspiration they need that pushes them to go after what they want in life too.
- **You're Going to Become More Understanding** - Self-care will make you a lot more compassionate towards yourself and the

people around you. The guilt is going to eventually fade away when you begin to understand the importance of self-care. You've heard of the term *"The straw that breaks the camel's back."* The straw keeps getting piled onto the camel until one day, a little piece of straw is enough to bring the entire pile crumbling down. That is what happens when you don't take the time to look after yourself. In any self-improvement journey, including one where you're learning to say "no" to others, you're going to make mistakes along the way. If you don't learn to forgive yourself for the mistakes, setbacks, and disappointments, you're not going to make any kind of positive progress in cultivating that mindset for success. Developing compassion for yourself gives you the opportunity to build the kind of mindset where you're focused on learning from your mistakes, rather than beating yourself up for it. You don't have to be perfect all the time, and you don't need to try and do it all. Trying to do too much without balancing it out by looking after yourself is going to be the straw that breaks in the camel's back.

- **You're Calmer** - When you're stressed, every little thing is going to set you off. The simplest things can trigger a lot of stress these days. Running late, getting stuck in traffic, getting an unexpected text message with less than thrilling news, your boss asking you to take on an extra assignment at the last minute when you're already rushing to meet a deadline. It's unfortunate that we experience stress, so often we don't even know the difference anymore. We've come to accept being stressed out as the new norm. It's even possible to feel stressed out at home these days. Maybe you felt stressed when you had to pay the bills earlier or while you were watching the news. Perhaps scrolling through social media made you feel stressed seeing pictures of your happy friends when your life feels like it's in chaos. When a friend texts you for a favor and you're reluctant to say yes because you would rather be relaxing at home. Life can quickly start to feel like it's becoming too much to handle when you're not looking after your mental, physical, and emotional wellbeing on top of everything else.

- **You're Not Going to Be Burned Out** - Nothing is going to stop you dead in your tracks like burnout. When you're burned out, *nothing can get done*. We don't take burnout quite as seriously as we should. Only when it happens, do we wake up and realize that something needs to be done. Only then do we realize that if things don't change, it is never going to get better. The problem with burnout is that it can happen with no warning. You're pushing, pushing, pushing, and then suddenly, everything feels like it's too much once you hit your limit. You won't see the burnout coming, and when it hits, it is going to hit you like a ton of bricks. Self-care is the only way to avoid that. When you need help, ask for it. It can be one of the strongest things that you do for yourself. Avoid the negative consequences of burnout *before* it happens by proactively looking after yourself.

Self-Care Tips to Becoming a More Confident Person

We live in stressful and sometimes crazy times. If we don't take the time to look after ourselves, it can really mess with our minds. The little things that you do for yourself can go a long way toward making a big difference in your life.

- **Cut Toxic People Out of Your Life** - This is probably the most important self-care thing you can do. Toxic people do nothing but breed negativity and bad vibes. Toxic relationships can quickly bring you down, and if you constantly let your emotions get in the way of your actions, you could be that toxic relationship. A damaged relationship is not always easy to repair, and to avoid damaging it at all in the first place; you need to always make it a habit to cut toxic people out of your life once and for all. Toxic personalities are only going to create more unnecessary drama in your life. This is the unforeseen toxicity, one that is going to leave you feeling miserable because toxic personalities are nothing more than a drain on your energy. Toxic personalities will never be truly happy, no matter what you do for them. There will always be a reason to complain, a reason why it is never good enough. They will hold you back and weigh you down in life, diminishing your confidence and belief in yourself. It can be difficult to leave once you've formed a bond with them, especially if you care about them. None of the confidence or self-esteem tips you've learned so far are going to be of any use to you if you still keep these toxic people around. They'll unravel any good that you do to try and boost your confidence. Cut them out and toss them out. You don't have to be their enemy, but you don't have to be their friend either. If you can't cut them out of your life completely for one reason or another, then the next best thing to do is to limit your contact with them. With toxic people, you need to have high standards. If someone is not treating you the way you deserve or value what you have to offer, then they're not suited to be in your life. It is as simple as that.
- **Keep A Journal** - This can have a huge impact on your emotional and mental wellbeing. Journals have served as an outlet for their owners to record all the personal emotions, ideas, thoughts, reflections, views, experiences, and more by allowing

them to privately document their thoughts in a "safe space," so to speak. That safe space is a journal that is meant for their eyes alone, and they can rest assured that no one else will be able to read their innermost thoughts unless they want them to. Journaling is a great way to help keep you on the right track towards being more mindful. You know that sense of relief that you get when you've successfully let your emotions out? That feeling that you get when you've confided in someone about everything that is bothering you and you feel as if a huge weight has been lifted off your shoulders? That's the same kind of effect that you get with journaling. Journaling promotes a state of mindfulness because when you're writing down all that you are feeling, you are acknowledging your thoughts and paying attention to them, really seeing them down on paper for the first time in a way you may not otherwise be able to if they are all just jumbled up in your mind. Instead of letting your mind wander, and your thoughts get out of control, writing them down in a response journal will force you to bring them into focus, especially when you ask yourself questions in the journal and then attempt to answer them.

- **Be Selfish With Your Time** - Your time is precious, and you should invest time in the things you want to do. Everyone deserves some alone time to recuperate, and if you feel that you need some time to yourself, take it. Take as much time off as you need, and don't let anyone make you feel bad about it. To avoid being overwhelmed, you must be selfishly protective of your time. If you don't, other people will always have more control over you than they should. They'll keep asking you for favors too if they know that you're not going to say no to them. Be selfish with your time. Spend it with yourself when you need to. Spend more time with people who bring out the best in you instead. You are not obligated to spend more time with the toxic person than you should. You're not obligated to keep saying yes and doing things for other people at the risk of neglecting your own needs. Don't feel about being selfishly protective of your time. This is something that must be done for the sake of your emotional wellbeing. Your quiet time is not something you should willingly compromise on. This is part of your self-care process and a way to balance your mental and physical wellbeing. Your quiet time routine can be anything that works for you. Go for a walk, stretch your muscles, spend time alone until you feel better, taking short breaks throughout the day to step away from people. Retreating to your quiet time is the easiest way to keep yourself from feeling emotionally exhausted, and quiet time can be done anywhere, and whenever you feel it.

- **Take A Step Back from Social Media** - Social media is fun, but it can also be a very toxic place to spend too much time in. Social media has a way of drawing us in and keeping us hooked for hours, but it isn't as relaxing as we think. When your mind is still absorbing some of the negativity you see on social media, that is not taking care of yourself. Unplugging from the media is essential to avoid overwhelming your senses. It's good to take a step back every now and then from the negativity, shock value, sensationalism, and extremely traumatic or emotional moments that certain content on social platforms can expose you to. None of which are good if they're overloading your senses. It doesn't help that we all have minds that are biased toward being attracted to the negative in the first place. Continuously feeding your mind with this type of content is only going to make it harder for you to find peace and balance, so avoid it whenever you can and choose to spend some quiet time alone instead. This is an outstanding self-care and survival practice that is going to help you thrive without feeling overwhelmed.
- **Set Boundaries** - Set boundaries because you need them. Without boundaries, people are always going to take advantage of you, even if they don't realize that they're doing it. Without boundaries, you're always going to have a hard time saying no to requests. Without boundaries, there can be no self-care. Healthy boundaries are your ultimate protection against being too overwhelmed. Protecting yourself and your own self-worth comes first, and you should never allow yourself to be emotionally bullied by anyone, no matter who they are. Do not let someone else make you feel that you are unworthy or inferior; this kind of behavior pattern is dangerous. Setting boundaries helps to protect yourself from them because it helps to limit how much influence they will have over your life. Setting boundaries can be in the form of limiting your time with them or finding a support system to help you manage your emotions after each encounter. It would depend on the situation you may be in. By defining your boundaries, you will come to understand what your limits are, and this will make it much easier for you to say no in favor of looking after yourself.
- **Exercise and Eat Right** - Sometimes, the simplest solutions can turn out to be the most effective. Physical exercise is the best relaxation technique out there for both your mind and body that won't cost you a thing. Your lifestyle habits play a big part in the current state of your stress levels. It is recommended that you exercise at least three to four times a week for 30-minutes per session. Perform moderate to intense exercises like jogging, brisk walking, cycling, hiking, or any form of aerobic activity that is

going to get your heart rate up. This gives your endorphin levels a boost, a hormone that helps you feel good and feel happy. The perfect antidote to combat stress. Don't forget to eat well too. The stress of everyday pressures may have had a disruptive effect on your eating patterns. Now that you are taking a more proactive role in your self-care routine, you can start making an effort to eat well again. Keep your mind sharp, and your body fit by eating a well- balanced diet that meets all their nutritional needs and steers clear of anything that is going to impact your body in a negative way. Take it a step further by combining it with an exercise routine too. Living a healthy lifestyle can do wonders for your mental and emotional health. You're going to start feeling really good about yourself because you like the results that you see in the mirror. When you know that you look good, you start to feel good. You're energetic, you're clear-minded, you feel good, and you feel like you are ready to take on any challenge that is thrust at you. You become a more confident person, and this is going to give your ability to say no a huge boost when you've got the confidence you need to back you up.

CONCLUSION

Thank you for making it through to the end of *Self-Confidence for Beginners*, let's hope it was informative and able to provide you with all of the tools you need to achieve your goals, whatever they may be.

You are an incredible person, and you have a lot to offer the world. Once you embrace this, it becomes so much easier to start building that confidence from within. Start building your confidence from within, and it will shine through externally. Confidence is going to be the difference as to whether you enjoy your life or live miserably. Now that you know the steps that must be taken to start working on building your confidence, the rest is up to you from this point forward. What is life if you don't enjoy it, right?

Choose today to be a positive person. With hard work, determination, and the right attitude, you can make all the steps in this book work for you. The confidence that you display in your life is going to change everything. It's going to show in your job, your relationships, even your finances. If you make the commitment to be confident, you're going to see results very quickly.

Finally, if you found this book useful in any way, a review on Amazon is always appreciated!

DESCRIPTION

To all the self-confidence seekers out there, you are not alone.
Life can seem significantly harder when you don't have confidence on your side. Confidence is something that you have to teach yourself over time. The only way to become the best version of yourself is through hard work, and that is what this process is. *Hard work,* but it is hard work that is going to be worth it when you see what a difference confidence makes in your life.

Confidence is something that is bigger than you. It is an unseen force that motivates you, supports you, pushes you to become the very best that you can be. It gives you the courage you need to face any challenge that comes your way. It strengthens your belief that you are good enough and worthy enough to achieve anything that you want in life. It lets you know that it is okay to fail because you have the strength and the resilience you need to pick yourself up again. It teaches you to recognize the opportunities that come into your life and gives you the courage to seize the moment before it slips through your fingers.

That is just a snippet of what a difference confidence can make in your life. Is it an easy skill to cultivate? Not all the time. Is it going to be worth it? Absolutely! Confidence is not something you're born with. It's a skillset. This is a skill set that you are about to learn in this book. *Self-Confidence* is packed with all the essential tips you need to get over those mental and emotional hurdles that have been holding you back in life for far too long.

Confidence is a journey that starts from within. It has to begin with a strong desire to be the change you want to see in your life. Nobody else can do it for you, and the good news is, you've already taken a step in the right direction when you stumbled upon this book. *Self-Confidence* will expose you to:

- How to drop your old mindset and begin to understand what confidence truly means.
- How to take the necessary steps to move out of your comfort zone.
- Why you need to expose yourself to challenges to grow.
- What you can do to effectively deal with your nervous anxiety because anxiety and confidence cannot exist side by side.
- Who your inner critic is, what it does, and how you can stomp it out for good, so it never holds you back again.
- Why tough personalities and characters are the ones that turn out to be the most confident of all.
- Why self-care is not selfish, and why you should never let anyone make you feel bad for taking the time you need to look after yourself.

Confidence truly is the key that makes a remarkable difference in your life. If you believe in yourself, the whole world will believe in you too. Perception is reality, and the secret to getting ahead in life is, really, no big secret at all. It's merely confidence. Are you ready to become a happier, fulfilled, confident person? Let's get right to it.

www.ingramcontent.com/pod-product-compliance
Lightning Source LLC
Chambersburg PA
CBHW071408070526
44578CB00002B/515